MARCHING ON

Companion volume

MARCHING ORDERS

MARCHING ON

Daily readings for younger people

by

WILLIAM BARCLAY

edited by
DENIS DUNCAN

HODDER AND STOUGHTON
LONDON SYDNEY AUCKLAND TORONTO
with
THE SAINT ANDREW PRESS
EDINBURGH

CONTENTS

MARCHING ON

If you have seen *Marching Orders*, you will have met Dr. William Barclay in my introduction there and in his "thoughts" in that book.

If, by any chance, you haven't discovered, till now, this amazing man, then I hope you will come to know him and love him through these further "thoughts" of his which I have reshaped and rewritten for you.

Your parents may like to know that this series is based mainly on material in my *Every Day with William Barclay*, published in October 1973 by Hodder and Stoughton.

Dr. Barclay is one of the most famous of Christian writers. You will find many of his books fascinating and inspiring in later life. But besides being a writer with (literally!) millions of books sold, he is a university teacher at Glasgow University, a TV broadcaster, a wonderful preacher, a choir conductor, a football supporter, a railway-engine enthusiast—and much more. He is an amazing man.

I have added a reading to each day's entry and tried as far as possible to avoid passages used in *Marching Orders*. If a verse figure ends like this, 18a, it means the reading ends after the first part of verse 18.

In rewriting these Barclay thoughts for you, it may be that on a few occasions, I have let a thought of my own slip in. You won't be able to spot these, but I hope Dr. Barclay will forgive this editorial licence! I have been so close to much of Dr. Barclay's material and thoughts for so long now, I am not always sure where he ends and I begin!

If the book, as a whole, gives *you* pleasure and profit, however, I hope he will be happy.

I shall!

DENIS DUNCAN

MONTH ONE

LAUGH!

"There was a little Indian girl at school today," announced my son proudly.

"Does she speak English?" I asked.

"No," came the reply, "But it doesn't matter because she laughs in English."

Laughter is the language of everyone, as this story told to me by a friend says so well.

You can laugh in any language and it will be understood.

There is of course the wrong kind of laughter. There is the laughter which laughs at the wrong things.

There is the laughter which can see something amusing in cruelty, or which can laugh at something which is unpleasant and dirty.

There is the laughter which laughs *at* a person and perhaps makes fun of his weaknesses.

Jesus, I am sure, made people laugh.

Try to imagine a camel struggling through a needle's eye.

Or a man with a huge plank in his eye worrying about a splinter in someone else's!

To be able to laugh at something is often to be able to learn from it.

There is "a time to laugh" says the Preacher in Ecclesiastes 3: 4.

There is—more often than we think!

Read St. Matthew 7: 1–5.

THE QUESTION WHY

Are you an "animated question mark"?

In other words are you always asking questions?

You should be!

For the way to learn is to ask.

Obviously I don't mean you must become a nuisance to people by popping all sorts of questions to them at awkward moments!

Of course not.

But I do mean that the right use of the word "Why?" *is* the way to learn.

Where was Jesus when his parents lost him in Jerusalem? He was found in the temple "surrounded by the teachers, listening to them *and putting questions*" (St. Luke 2: 46, N.E.B.).

Keep asking!

Politely, of course.

But keep asking. You will learn of man, the world *and* God that way.

Read Proverbs 1: 1–9.

SELF-MADE?   Day Three

Sometimes you will hear someone say, "I'm a self-made man."

Unfortunately it is often an arrogant thing to say.

And in any case, it just isn't true.

None of us are really "self-made".

But we can do certain things to make ourselves more useful to people and to God.

We can add to our education our *self*-education.

That is why the asking of questions about which we thought yesterday is so important.

It is the way to learn.

So how can we learn?

We can learn from good advice we are given—by our parents, our teachers, our friends.

We can learn from examples we are shown by people we love and admire.

We can learn from our mistakes.

We can learn from our experience of the world and of God.

You can teach yourself a lot if you try.

Read Proverbs 7: 11–14.

IT'S GOOD TO KNOW! Day Four

A certain firm had installed a very complicated machine in its works. One day the machine went wrong. The firm's own mechanics were unable to deal with the fault, so they sent out an emergency call for help to the makers of the machine.

An engineer arrived. He looked at the machine. Then he seemed to do no more than give a part of it a light tap with a hammer and the machine was going as well as ever again!

At the end of the month the account came in. It read, "To repairing the machine—£5·67½".

This seemed a very large sum to charge for carrying out such a simple repair: one tap with a hammer!

The firm wrote to the makers of the machine asking them how this sum of £5·67½ had been estimated. They got a reply, but possibly not the one they expected. It read, "To mechanic's time in repairing machine—67½p; to knowing how to do it—£5·00".

It is knowing how to do something that is so important. If you want to get on in life, then to get knowledge of *how* things are done is very important.

And this is true also of the Christian life. You must get to know *how* to live as a Christian.

We learn best, of course, through Jesus who is the way and the life.

Read St. John 3: 7–21.

THE NAMELESS ONES

Alistair Maclean writes in *High Country*:

"I read a tale set in jewels the other day. It was of Luther marching through the streets of Worms to that mighty conflict in which the fate of the Reformation was finally decided. The streets were crowded. The multitudes were silent. The leader of the new Faith pressed steadily, almost stonily, on. Suddenly a voice, clear as a bell, rang through the air. 'Play the man, play the man. Fear not death. It can but slay the body. There is a life beyond.' It was noticed thereafter that the face of Captain Greatheart shone."

We know the names of the great saints and martyrs, but there are thousands upon thousands of simple men and women, whose names are forgotten, but who chose to die rather than to deny their Lord.

It is on the nameless ones that the Church is built.

We owe the Reformation, our Church and all it means, to the cry of encouragement of a nameless witness, when Luther's heart was near to shrinking from its task.

The Church is built on the witness of a nameless crowd of faithful people.

We benefit from what others before us have done. So *other people* must benefit from *our* efforts.

Because we have learned so much from the witness of nameless people, we too must bear our witness in such a way that we may make it easier for others to follow Christ.

In Jesus's army, we may not be the leaders and the generals about whom everyone will talk. But we can at

14

least be the ordinary soldiers, whose names are unknown, but on whose valour the outcome of the battle must depend.

It is *not* important that our names be known.
It *is* important that we play our part.

Read St. John 21: 15.

SPARROWS

Railway stations don't always have cafeterias! I think they are improving, but I remember one at Manchester Exchange Station (this is quite a long time ago) which wasn't very good. It was just a makeshift counter and one or two uncomfortable forms. But it was a pleasure to have a cup of tea and a sandwich there!

Why?

Because the station sparrows shared it with you! They were so tame that they hopped about on the counter and came within inches of you to pick up your crumbs and eat them!

I shall always remember the friendly sparrows in Manchester Exchange Station.

A minister friend once told me another story about sparrows.

He said that he had been with his wife on holiday in Paris. He went into the Bois de Boulogne—a great park in that city. There he saw a man feeding the sparrows.

The man had a long French loaf in his hand. He would break off a piece, crumble it between his finger and thumb, and the sparrows would fly on to his hand and eat the bread. The strange thing was that the sparrows seemed almost to queue in single file, coming one at a time for their crumbs!

It all sounds rather far-fetched, I know, but he assured me it was true!

Once, he told me, two sparrows flew up together, and

15

tried to get at the same crumb. The man looked at one of the sparrows and tut-tutted (in French, of course!) and, lo and behold, the sparrow went back to its place in the queue!

Then the man spoke soothingly and the queue-jumping sparrow came up to get his piece of bread!

My friend asked the man how he managed to tame the sparrows to this extent. He said that, for years and years at lunch-time, he had been coming to feed the sparrows, and they had simply got to know him and were no longer frightened of him.

My friend also made this interesting comment. He noticed that man's fingers particularly. Like many Frenchmen, he was rather dark-skinned. But the finger and thumb with which he crumbled the bread were quite white. They had been whitened by the bread, and scarred with the pecks that the birds had given him.

I rather like that story of the sparrows.

I'm glad Jesus found he could use them in parables, too, to help us understand his teaching.

Read St. Matthew 10: 29–31.

JESUS AND THE SPARROWS   Day Seven

Let's look at what Jesus said about sparrows. Matthew and Luke report it with significant differences.

St. Matthew says, "Are not two sparrows sold for a farthing? And one of them shall not light on the ground without your Father knowing." (Matthew 10: 29).

Incidentally, it's not a case of the sparrow falling down *dead*. It's rather the picture of a sparrow hopping on the ground. God is aware even of that.

St. Luke has it, "Are not five sparrows sold for two farthings, and not one of them is forgotten before God?" (Luke 12: 6).

Is there something wrong with the arithmetic here? *Two* sparrows for *one* farthing and *five* sparrows for *two* farthings? Someone seems to have slipped up, hasn't he?

No! In Palestine then two sparrows did cost one farthing, but if you were prepared to spend two farthings, an *extra* sparrow was given you for nothing. A sparrow was, literally, worth nothing; that extra one could be thrown in without any worry. Yet God sees and cares for *that* sparrow!

Jesus used that saying for a good reason. If, he said, God cares for a sparrow like that: if God cares even for the sparrow that is worth *nothing at all*, the one that is just added on to the bargain and given away as worthless, how much more will he care for you?

God cares for every sparrow.
Are *you* not of much more value than many sparrows?
I'm sure you know you are!

Read St. Luke 12: 1–9.

SCRAPING AN ACQUAINTANCE   Day Eight

Do you know this phrase, "To scrape an acquaintance"? Well, this is, I believe, how that curious phrase was created.

In the ancient world of Greece and Rome, the public baths were the places where everyone met. The noble *and* the man-in-the-street met there. The baths were much more like clubs than places where you went to wash. It all seems a bit strange to us, but this is just a fact of history.

It was there too that the gymnasts trained. It was there that philosophers like Plato met and talked to their friends and discussed life's problems.

These Roman baths give us the explanation of this phrase.

One day the Roman Emperor Hadrian visited the baths. In those days bathers used scrapers to scrape off the oil with which they anointed their bodies after bathing.

In the baths Hadrian happened to see an old soldier. The old man was too poor to buy a proper scraper normally made of bone or ivory or metal. So he was having to use an old piece of broken pottery as a scraper.

Hadrian said nothing, but that night he sent the old veteran a sum of money, not only to buy a scraper, but also to help him with his poverty.

The story of the Emperor's generosity soon became widely known. Word went round, therefore, that Hadrian was to visit the baths again. When he arrived, the baths were crowded with bathers and they were all using pieces of broken pottery to scrape themselves, in the hope of arousing the Emperor's generosity again!

Hadrian looked at them and smiled gently. "Scrape on, gentlemen," he said, "you will not scrape an acquaintance with me!"

It is from that incident that we get our phrase "scraping an acquaintance" with someone, which means trying to get to know someone usually for rather selfish reasons!

I think this incident has something to say about genuine giving.

Can you think what?

Read St. Mark 14: 3–9.

THE LINGUIST   **Day Nine**

A Welsh girl went to work in an English town.

In that English city there was a Welsh church, but it was

a long journey from where the girl worked and stayed. Nevertheless, each Sunday she made the long journey in order to worship with her own people and in her own tongue.

The people with whom the girl stayed and worked were kindly people, so they invited her to save herself all the trouble of that long Sunday journey and to come with them to their own church. But the girl courteously declined the invitation. She said she would rather make the longer journey in order to share in worship *in the tongue which she knew so well and loved so much.*

The master of the house was puzzled. Very gently and in no attitude of criticism, he said to the girl, "You must remember that Jesus wasn't a Welshman!"

The girl answered, "I know that, sir, *but it is in Welsh that he speaks to me.*"

Jesus is the greatest "linguist" in the world!

He speaks to us all in our own language, whatever that language is.

Do you remember what happened on the day of Pentecost?

On that day what amazed the people more than anything else was that every man heard the message of the gospel *in his own tongue* (Acts 2: 8).

Jesus Christ speaks *our* language.

He speaks the language of *everyone else too.*

His gospel can be translated into every possible dialect and accent, because, whatever words we happen to use, that gospel is the same.

It meets everyone's needs.

It is for all people—everywhere.

Read Acts 2: 1–12.

Let's think a bit more about this idea of Jesus as a linguist, the man who "speaks" in many languages.

Jesus speaks to men of every nation.

Christianity is something that crosses all national boundaries. The Church does not belong to one land or nation or continent or colour.

Within the Church all nations are gathered. In His Kingdom, there is "one fold and one shepherd".

Jesus comes to everyone in that man's own tongue.

Jesus speaks to people of every kind and condition.

The philosopher with all his wisdom; the simple man who has no book-learning; the great man with the cares of great affairs upon him; the humble man of whom no one has ever heard; the saint who is holy; the sinner who is conscious of wrong—Jesus speaks to each and all in a language they can understand.

No matter what the problem, Jesus has something to say that will help.

Jesus speaks to people of every experience.

The person who has succeeded, the person who has failed; the individual whose dreams have come true, the individual whose dream can never be realised; the child; the youth; the middle-aged; the elderly; the man for whom the sun shines in joy, the woman for whom life is wet with the tears of sorrow—Jesus speaks to each and all in a language they understand.

Why? Because the language Jesus speaks is the language of love.

The wise men ask, "What language did Christ speak?"
   They cavil, argue, search, and little prove.
O sages, leave your Syriac and your Greek!
Each heart contains the knowledge that you seek.
   Christ spoke the universal language—Love.

It is the wonder of Jesus that he speaks to every man in his *own* tongue.

He is, truly, *the* spiritual linguist.

Read Ephesians 4: 1–6.

SPILLED MILK   Day Eleven

Have you heard the famous fable of Perette and her milkpail? It is one of the oldest fables in the world.

You will find it in books by French writers like Lafontaine, in Rabelais, and even in the *Arabian Nights*, which comes from a different region.

Perette worked on a farm. One day the farmer's wife gave her a pailful of milk for herself. So Perette put the pail of milk on her head (you carried things on your head in those days!) and she set off to the market to sell it.

As Perette walked and walked she began dreaming her dreams.

Perette's dream went something like this.

"I'll sell this pail of milk. With the money I get for it, I'll buy some eggs, and I'll soon have some chicks. I'll keep them and I'll fatten them, and when they are grown into hens, I'll sell them. And with the money I get for the hens, I'll buy a little pig. I'll keep him and I'll fatten him and I'll sell him."

Then she began to smile as she thought of this prospect.

"And with the money I get for the pig, I'll buy a real silk dress. I'll put on my dress, and I'll go to the dance. Robin will be there. When he sees me all dressed in silk, he'll ask me to marry him. But I'll show him how particular I am; I'll toss my head and . . ."

And there and then, in her dream, she tossed her head, as she would do at Robin! And, of course, when she tossed her head, off fell the pail, and the milk all spilled.

All Perette's dreams were gone.

21

There's a lot to think about in the story of Perette and her dreams, isn't there?

Read St. Luke 12: 13–21.

DREAMING DREAMS   Day Twelve

Did you think about yesterday's story of Perette? I hope so, because it has its lessons for our lives.

Here is the first.
We must dream sometimes!
It was very sad in the days of Eli that there was "no open vision" in the land (1 Sam. 3: 1). There was a lack of real inspiration because people were out of touch with God.

The writer of the Proverbs puts it like this, "Where there is no vision, the people will perish" (Prov. 29: 18). This is really a wrong translation! But even if it is an accidental phrase, it contains a great truth.

People who have done great things have had their dreams —dreams of distant places, dreams of a new world, dreams of overcoming pain, dreams of harnessing new power, like nuclear power. There is *a dream* behind every great action.

But here is the second point.
The dream needs an interpreter.
The complaint of Pharaoh's butler and baker, when they were in prison, was, "We have dreamed a dream and there is no interpreter of it" (Gen. 40: 8). Dreams do often have meanings and the interpretation of a dream can make a big difference to you. One person's dream may drive him to *selfish* ambition or it may move him to *selfless* ambition or it may move him to *selfless service*. It all depends how you interpret the dream.

The vividness of the dream may drive you to despair or to heroic action. It again all depends *how* you interpret it.

22

So let your dreams be dreams that will help you serve people better.

Jesus is, in a sense, the centre of all our dreams as Christians. We want to be *like* him; to be *with* him; to be *for* him.

If *he* is our dream, *we* are bound to be a blessing to many.

Read Genesis 40.

DREAMS INTO ACTION   Day Thirteen

There is more to say about dreams.
Think about this!
When a man has had the dream and found the interpretation of it, the first thing that the dream needs is action.
In other words, dreams don't realise themselves. Dreams remain just a vision in our mind *until we add action to them.*

This is where the test comes for all of you. Your dream may come in a flash, but the turning of the dream into reality may take more than half a lifetime! All your life may be an effort to make a dream come true.

But let me warn you about this.
The road to the fulfilment of your life's dream will be through sweat and toil. The greater your dream, the longer and the harder will be the road to it.

So let's just go over these thoughts about dreams again.
First you must have a dream of what you want to do, then—as it can take the wrong way unless you interpret it rightly—you need the right interpretation.
The realisation of the dream may take a long, long time. It is much easier to sit dreaming than it is to start working!

If you only sit dreaming, in the end you will get nowhere!

23

But if you work, toil, persevere and sacrifice, you will be very happy, for you will be the person whose dream came true!

I hope all your dreams do come true!
If they are the right dreams, we shall all be blessed!

Read Joel 2: 28–32.

WHAT'S THE POINT?   Day Fourteen

"What is the point?"

That is a very sensible question for you to ask, for you will find, as you grow up, that you are doing many pointless things! You must, in life, make a decision on *how* you will spend time. We can't do *everything*, so it is important to be sure that what we are doing makes *the best use of our time*.

So let's ask this question: "What is the point of . . . ?"

What is the point of so much of our hurry and our worry, our effort and our anxiety?

We see people working so hard to get a little more money, doing double time, overtime, perhaps two or three jobs. We can watch people being cruel and selfish and unkind just to get themselves one step further up the ladder. *What is the point* of it all? What good is it really going to do us to live like that?

We worry about this, that and the next thing—but is it all sensible concern? Are the things we are worrying about going to do us—or the world, or people—good? *What is the point* about it all?

Even if the things we worry about do happen, the heavens won't necessarily collapse. As a friend of mine often says, "It will be all the same a hundred years from now." Often it will be like that.

So it is useful sometimes to ask this question: *"What is the point* of what I am doing?"

24

I must say I do sometimes wonder what the point is of many of the arguments that go on in many church committees! People get so upset and bothered about the placing of a comma in a report! I have often been at committees that spent hours arguing over very trivial questions.

We could save time and trouble and ill-feeling, too, if, before we started an argument, we just asked, "*What is the point* of it, anyhow?"

If there is a point, it is worth an argument!

If it isn't, we ought to use the time and effort for a better purpose!

Read Jude 16–20.

THE POINT OF LIFE   Day Fifteen

Let's just ask that question, "What is the point?" again.

First, there is a very significant comment from an ancient writer and philosopher called Epictetus. He said, "*Vain is the discourse of philosophy by which no human heart is healed.*"

That is something for you to think about. Argument that takes place *for its own sake* is pointless. If our discussions will lead to helping people, then there is value in them. But talking for talking's sake just has no point!

There is a bigger question still to answer. It is this: "*What is the point of life?*"

For me, the point of life is to know Jesus and through Him to be ready, fearlessly, to meet the call of God whenever that call comes. If we see life in that context, then everything else will fall into place.

Do you remember that story of Elijah? He once ran away when things were very difficult. Out in the desert there came God's voice to him, "What doest thou here, Elijah?" (1 Kings 19: 9).

25

"What's the point?" God was saying to Elijah. You are very worked up, he said, and sorry for yourself. But what's it all about?

We shall all be able to see better what things are important and what things really don't matter, if we can sometimes just stop, and think, and ask that question, "Now, *what's the point* of this?"

See if you can do that sometime!

Read Philippians 3: 1–7.

KEEP QUIET! Day Sixteen

I once knew a man of whom it was said that he could speak seven different languages, but that he could also *be silent in seven languages!*

There are times when we ought to keep silent.
Don't you agree?
Let's think of some of these times.

We ought to keep silent when we are angry.

If we speak when we are really angry, we shall almost certainly say things which will hurt others. And we shall regret these things bitterly when we remember them.

I have known many a friendship to have been wrecked because one person said too much. Many a friendship has been saved, because someone knew how to "hold his tongue" in the moment of anger.

Count ten—in silence—before you speak in anger!

We ought to keep silent when we want to criticise.

It is so easy to criticise! But most criticisms are better left unsaid. No one really has the right to criticise at all, unless he himself is prepared to try to do as well as the person criticised.

It is a good rule never to be slow with praise and never to be quick with criticism.

Try it out!

We ought to keep silent when we are criticised.

It is easy to criticise, but not so easy to accept criticism! It is a natural instinct to jump to our own defence! But that is the very thing that can lead to quarrels and create hurts which are hard to heal.

Pills and criticism are sometimes hard to swallow, but sometimes both of them can do us good!

Anaximenes, the old Cynic philosopher, used to say that there are only two people who can tell us the truth. The first is "an enemy who hates us bitterly" and the second "a friend who loves us dearly".

The truth can hurt.

It is sometimes better to hold our peace and just bear with situations we would like to criticise, in silence.

If the truth *must* be spoken, let the truth be given but only *in love*.

Read St. Matthew 26: 57–63a.

COMPENSATIONS   Day Seventeen

There is a Glasgow church in which I have sometimes preached. The organist in that church was blind.

It has always amazed me that you only needed to tell him once the hymns you wanted to sing.

He knows the whole order of service, too! You can't hand him a list. He couldn't read it. But you simply repeat the hymn-list once, and it is firm in his memory.

I was preaching there one morning, and with me was the minister of the church. After I had fixed up the morning list of hymns with this amazing blind man, the minister was arranging the evening praise list.

The minister said, "I would like this evening to have the hymn 'For those we love within the veil'. That's hymn number 216." "No," said the blind organist in his soft Highland voice, "not 216, 218."

This blind man actually carried in his memory the number of every hymn in the hymn book!

When I spoke to him about his amazing memory, he said it wasn't amazing at all! He simply regarded the gift of memory as a compensation for his blindness.

And to him that good memory was indeed a blessing.

Isn't it marvellous that when people lose (or don't have) one faculty, they are specially blessed over another?

How marvellous is (as I would call it) *the principle of compensation*.

Read St. John 9: 1–25.

ANYTHING YOU CAN DO ...   Day Eighteen

I once visited a youth fellowship, in what we call one of the Church Extension churches, on the south side of Glasgow. There must have been at least 200 young people there, many of them from a housing estate which is said to be rather a tough spot.

I always received a good hearing from that group.

One of those who asked me questions was a young lad who was a spastic.

It was an amazing thing that this boy with his handicap could take part in a discussion like that. What moved me most was that he would say how he prayed to God to help him to conquer his handicap. And God had helped him most amazingly, he insisted.

I talked to the boy afterwards, and he told me he had

28

only one ambition and that was to be a minister. Then he said, "I'll bet you I can do something *you* can't do."

I said, "I wouldn't be surprised at that. What *can* you do?"

He said, "I can read a page of any newspaper once, and then repeat it by heart."

He could!

If that boy ever becomes a minister, he has a gift that is going to be of tremendous value to him.

Isn't this another case of *the principle of compensation* I spoke about yesterday? I think it is.

If something is taken away, something else is given in extra measure. Much had been taken from the spastic lad, as it was from the blind organist, but they both had amazing memories.

I find that very thrilling.
Don't you?

Read 2 Corinthians 11: 21b–31.

MY COMPENSATION   Day Nineteen

I am deaf: in fact so deaf that without a very wonderful hearing aid, I cannot hear anyone!

But there is one tremendous advantage in being deaf. If you are deaf, your power of concentration is far more than doubled, for the very simple reason that you don't hear all the sounds which are so distracting for other people!

I find there is a real compensation for a writer in being deaf!

If God has taken something from us, he gives us something else. This is the great lesson of *the principle of compensation.* Count your blessings rather than brood on your losses!

That was one of the great discoveries that Paul made.

Paul was a sick man, a man with a trouble which was like a "stake" (2 Cor. 12: 7, it is a "stake" rather than a "thorn") turning and twisting in his body.

He prayed to God to take that terrible pain away. He did this again and again. It wasn't taken away. But out of that terrible experience of pain and agony, which was to haunt him all his life, Paul discovered something. He found what he calls "the grace which is sufficient for all things" was there to help him in his weakness (2 Cor. 12: 1–10).

If we can look on things in that way, we shall find that life is full of compensations.

I have proved that!

Read 2 Corinthians 12: 1–12.

SEPARATION   Day Twenty

I am not often alone. But once I was quite alone for what seemed a long time. Holidays and other things separated me from my family. They were in Canada.

What made it worse was the fact that there was a postal strike in Canada, so I could not even be in touch with my wife by letter!

All this has made me think about being alone!

First, there is *the feeling of loneliness.*

There were other people round about me in Oxford (where I was at the time) but, as you might say, they were not *my* people.

Do you remember what Queen Victoria said after the death of Albert, the Prince Consort, the husband on whom she depended and to whom she was so devoted? "There is no one," she said, "to call me 'Victoria' now." No one could call the Queen by her own name except Albert. And he was dead.

If you are separated from parents or friends, it is a lonely feeling.

I have learned a lot from feeling like this! I now understand a little better *how* it feels to be lonely.

I can also understand how it feels to be a stranger in a strange place. And I can see some of the temptations that come when you are lonely.

I can understand Dick Sheppard's actions, for instance.

Have you heard of Dick Sheppard? He was a London vicar and very well-known many years ago. It was said that, when he was left alone, he used to leave the rectory and spend the night in an hotel, not specially to speak to anyone, but simply to feel that there were people there in the lounge, and that through the bedroom wall there was someone else!

You learn a lot when you have to be alone.

I am sure you are not unlucky enough to be lonely. But I think you will understand how lonely *I* felt! And because of that, I'm sure *you* will want to help lonely people.

Read St. Mark 14: 32–42.

"I WANT REAL PEOPLE"   Day Twenty-one

Did you hear about the little girl who did not want to be left alone when she was put to bed? She wanted someone to sit with her.

"You've got your doll," said her mother. "Your doll will keep you company."

"When I'm lonely," the little girl replied, "a doll is no good to me. I want someone with skin on her face."

That was a very true answer, wasn't it? When we are lonely, we like real people beside us.

31

Perhaps this will help you to think of poor people, old people, refugee people, and other lonely people. They too want more than our words. They want the love and friendship of real people.

Jesus said, "Inasmuch as you did it unto one of the least of these, my brethren, you did it unto me."

God comes to help people—*through* other people.
People with skin on their faces.
Real people.
Like me.
Like you.

And of course God came to help us through a real person. Jesus.

Read St. Matthew 9: 18–26.

ORDINARY THINGS   Day Twenty-two

In his book called *The Aristocrats*, Roy Perrott tells of a man who was a miner, but became a peer of the realm.

In spite of his elevation to such a high position, he stayed on in the little humble house in which he had always lived and he did just what he had always done. He had no elaborate family treasures.

Roy Perrott says this about him, "The only significant family trophy he possessed was the old coal-pick which he had once used underground. Polished up to a silvery brightness, like some nobleman's escutcheon, it hung between two curtain-hooks on the parlour wall!"

The ex-miner peer was proud of *his* coal-pick, the tool of *his* trade.

A very fine thinker, scholar and teacher called L. P. Jacks used to tell how he wrote in the days before typewriters had become part of an author's equipment. In *his* time

32

everything was hand-written with pen and ink. (I mentioned him before, in *Marching Orders*, page 153.)

As he sat at his desk, he wore an old jacket, and the sleeve of the jacket was frayed at the place where it had constantly rubbed along his desk as he wrote. He said that, if he had to take something to God to justify his life, the one thing he would take would be the old jacket with the frayed sleeve.

What are the things *we* would most want to show to God?

Surely the ordinary things we use to do good and to help people.

We should be proud of good "ordinary" things.

Read St. Luke 24: 13–35.

SOMEONE'S WATCHING!   Day Twenty-three

I stepped off a bus, my journey over.

Without thinking what I was doing, I threw my ticket away.

I was hurrying away when I saw an old man who had stepped off the same bus. He too had a bus ticket, but *he* didn't throw his away. He walked over to the little wire basket attached to the nearest lamp-post and dropped his ticket in.

I felt I really was a "litter-lout", so I picked mine up from the gutter and placed it in the litter basket!

Doesn't a good example do something for us?

Human nature is easily influenced.

King Edward VIII accidentally left the bottom button of his waistcoat unfastened, and, before very long, every well-dressed man was doing the same!

A certain statesman wears a distinctive kind of coat (as

Mr. Harold Wilson does) and soon the coat becomes the uniform of the well-dressed business man!

A certain film star adopts a hair-style, and soon everyone is copying it!

A certain comedian produces a catchword, and soon everybody is using it!

A certain "royal" uses a gesture, and soon everyone is copying the prince or princess!

Example is one of the most powerful forces in this world. So it's important that *we* should set a good one.

Read 1 Timothy 4: 12–16.

ON THE MARCH AGAIN   Day Twenty-four

Have you heard that moving story of an incident in Dunkirk in the Second World War? I did refer to it briefly in *Marching Orders*, but I would like to tell the story more fully here.

On the quay of an English port, a number of French troops had been disembarked. The spirit had gone out of them, and they were lying there in a dull lethargy of despair. They knew that they had lost not a campaign, but their country.

Another ship came in, and from it there disembarked a detachment of the Brigade of Guards. The Guards' discipline had never relaxed. As far as it was possible, their uniform was still perfect and their equipment just as it ought to be.

On the quay they formed up, and marched away as if they had been changing the guard.

Some of the Frenchmen looked up listlessly. Then slowly a light began to be reborn in their eyes. Stiffly they rose, squared their shoulders, and marched off after the Guards. Before that movement had finished, every one of the Frenchmen had fallen in and was on the march.

This is the power of an example.

It had changed dispirited, defeated men into men who had got back their hope and their self-respect.

Read St. John 13: 1–17.

MAKE IT EASIER! Day Twenty-five

Someone is watching *you*—for sure!

The little boy watches the big boy, and models himself upon him.

The child watches his father or mother, and unconsciously copies his or her mannerisms and actions.

The Sunday-school scholar watches his or her teacher.

Do you remember how the Pied Piper of Hamelin piped the children away? As someone has said, "Everyone pipes for the feet of someone to follow."

When St. Paul was writing to Titus, he told him what to say to other people about their Christian duty. He goes on, "In all things show yourself a pattern, a type, an example of good works" (Titus 2: 7).

When he writes to Timothy, he says, "Be thou an example to the believers, in word, in conduct, in love, in spirit, in faith, in purity" (1 Tim. 4: 12).

Here is our responsibility.

A careless action of ours may make it easier for someone else to do something wrong, though we may never know about it.

A right action of ours may make it easier for someone to stay on the right road—and again we may never know it.

As St. Peter puts it, Jesus left us "an example, that we should follow his steps" (1 Peter 2: 21), and he left us the responsibility of being such that others can follow in ours.

In all we do we are making it easier or harder for someone else to do the right.

Make it easier, won't you?

Read 1 Peter 2: 19–24.

BE GENEROUS!   Day Twenty-six

My wife suffered at one time from that painful illness called fibrositis. She attended a city clinic in Glasgow for treatment.

She had many talks with an old lady who came to the clinic from the other side of the city.

One day, the old lady asked my wife if she could lend her a penny. This was some time ago as you will see!

You see, in the afternoon, old-age pensioners were able to have a concession fare on the trams. The old lady had nothing but one pound note. She wanted the penny to pay her fare home on the tram because she did not want to upset the conductress by offering her a pound note for a penny fare.

My wife opened her purse and gave the old lady the penny she needed. Then, laughingly, my wife pointed at all the money she happened to have in her purse at the moment —a ten-shilling note and two florins—and said, as a joke, "Look! That's all I've got until Tuesday (this happened on a Friday) when I get my housekeeping money."

The old lady's reaction was immediate. She held out the pound note. "Take this, dear," she said. "It'll help you over the week-end anyway, and you can give it back when you get your money."

Here was an old lady, an old-age pensioner, offering her *only* pound note to someone she hardly knew, because she thought that the stranger was worse off than herself.

Generosity is a great quality.

36

Always try to be generous.

And be ready with your generosity as soon as it is seen to be needed.

Read Acts 5: 1–11.

RICHES—THROUGH POVERTY   Day Twenty-seven

St. James, in his epistle, speaks of God who gives generously to all men, and never grudges the gift (James 1 : 5).

St. Paul speaks of the Lord Jesus Christ who, though he was rich, "yet for your sakes he became poor that ye through his poverty might be rich" (2 Cor. 8: 9).

It is not a case of giving big gifts. The size of a gift is really of no importance at all.

At the Feast of Purim the Jews have a lovely custom. It is laid down that at that Feast, which is the time of the giving of gifts, even the poorest person must search for someone poorer than himself and give him a gift.

Isn't that a lovely idea?

You never end up with less by being generous.

You always get something back.

Be generous!

Always!

Read 2 Corinthians 8: 1–15.

THEY SAW THE NEED   Day Twenty-eight

Here are two very interesting incidents. I found them in the life stories of great Christians.

The first comes from Ernest W. Bacon's biography of the famous preacher, Dr. Charles Spurgeon.

Dr. Spurgeon founded a college in which students might be trained for the ministry. It was a big undertaking, but he accomplished it.

One of the earliest students, the Rev. D. J. Hiley, tells of a meeting with Spurgeon when he was a student in that college.

They met one day in the corridor.

"Is that your best coat?" Spurgeon asked.

"Yes, sir," Hiley answered.

Spurgeon was silent for a moment. "I wonder if you would render me a little service," he said.

Hiley said that he would be delighted to render the great Dr. Spurgeon any service he could.

Spurgeon asked him to deliver a note at a certain tailor's shop.

Hiley goes on, "I was to wait for an answer. For reply— the tailor measured me for a new suit of clothes and an overcoat, and sent me away with a hat-box!"

You see what had happened?

Spurgeon had seen that the poor student needed a coat, a suit and a hat, and he *did* something about it!

The other incident comes from Richard Collier's biography of William Booth, although the story itself is about Bramwell Booth, when Bramwell had succeeded his father as General of the Army.

Collier writes, "The Army . . . had become his life . . . His officers' welfare was always paramount; once, lynx-eyed as always, he noticed that several officers taking tea with him bit on only one side of their jaws. Promptly, at his own expense, he sent them to his dentist."

Bramwell Booth saw that his officers needed dental treatment and he saw that they got it.

Dr. Spurgeon and Bramwell Booth both saw need and responded to it.

Immediately.

If you see someone in need, when you grow older, try to do something for him at once.

In doing that, *you* will be blessed.

Read St. Matthew 9: 35–38.

ACT!   **Day Twenty-nine**

Let's look a little more at these two great men, Dr. Spurgeon and Bramwell Booth.

Dr. Spurgeon was a great preacher, but he was also a great pastor. At one time he had 6,000 members in his church, and he claimed to know them all, not only by face, but even by name!

Bramwell Booth's diary shows that, in an average year, he granted at least 1,000 interviews.

However much immersed in administration Bramwell might be, or however high on the heights in his sermon preparation Spurgeon might be, neither of these great men was ever too busy to see people.

But these great men didn't just see people casually. They noticed what people needed.

Dr. Spurgeon at once noticed that threadbare coat, and Bramwell Booth at once noticed that need of dental treatment.

They did not simply look *at* people. They looked further and saw their needs.

We do not always notice when something is wrong. Too often we are not interested enough, we are not sensitive enough, we are not perceptive enough, we are not sympathetic enough to see signs of sorrow or of worry or of need in people we meet.

But a true Christian should have eyes to see his fellow man's need.

Here is something for you to aim at when you grow up.

39

Learn to understand when people have problems and need help.

St. James saw long ago that there is no point in seeing someone cold and hungry and in speaking words of pious good wishes, without doing anything practical to help (James 2: 15, 16).

To see need and to help need should be absolutely simultaneous.

You will do a lot for the world if you can do that!

And after all, doesn't God do this for us?

He sees our need and he helps us.

He sent Jesus to be with us.

He acted.

If *we* are going to reflect God's way, we shall *act* too!

Read St. Mark 1: 29–34.

IT WORKS! Day Thirty

I know a small boy whose father is a minister and who is also very interested—as indeed all sensible people are—in railway engines (I am, anyway!).

It so happened that where this little boy lived, a new church was being built.

He and his father were train-spotting one day, and a magnificent new engine appeared.

The father pointed out to the boy—I am not quite sure that the figures are absolutely accurate, but that does not matter too much—that the engine had cost about £60,000 to build. Said his father, "That's as much as the new church cost."

The boy thought for a minute and said, "Well, I would rather have the engine. I think that it's worth the money far more than the church."

"How do you make that out?" his father asked him.

"Well," said the boy, "the engine works!"

The real test of anything is, "Does it work?" Or, as Jesus puts it, "You will know them by their fruits" (Matt. 7: 20).

This is the test of a church.

Does a church send its members into the community to live for God and to live for men, or does it heap them into a building?

Does it raise barriers, or does it destroy barriers?

Does it unite Christians, or does it separate Christians?

Does it send out people whose lives are like "lights in a dark place" (Philippians 2: 15), or does it send out people whose lives discourage rather than attract?

This is the test of our lives too, isn't it?

If we really have the spirit of Jesus in us, we shall be a great blessing to our parents, our friends, and other people.

We shall be known by what we do, by whether our faith works or not.

Read St. Matthew 7: 15–23.

THE BETRAYER   Day Thirty-one

Sometimes I have had to go to towns and cities which I don't know at all. I have had to stop strangers to ask them the way to where I am going.

Now here is an interesting thing.

I can usually tell something about those people just by the directions they give me!

Usually people say that when you see such-and-such a place, you will be near your destination. Naturally, directions are given in relation to landmarks which stand out in *their* minds.

If a man says to me, "When you see such-and-such a church, you are getting near where you want to go," I know that man is a churchman! Because he directs me in terms of churches.

41

If he says, "You will see such-and-such a cinema on your left," I know that that man is a cinema-goer, because he directs me in terms of cinemas.

If he says to me, "You get off the bus after such-and-such a garage," that man is a motorist!

If he tells me that I must make for such-and-such a public-house, I know that he knows "pubs" well, because he directs me in terms of places like that.

So very often the directions a man gives give him away!

Our speech betrays us, doesn't it?
That is worth thinking about.

Read St. Luke 22: 54–62.

MONTH TWO

In Cheltenham, in the south-west of England, there was at one time an inn called "The Five Alls". It had a most interesting sign.

On the sign there was a king, with the motto: "I rule for all".

There was a bishop, with the motto: "I pray for all".

There was a lawyer, with the motto: "I plead for all".

There was a soldier, with the motto: "I fight for all".

And there was an artisan in working clothes, with the motto: "I work for all".

I think we could all learn a lot from that sign!

I rule for all.

If you should ever happen to be in control of many people, as you may be in *your* job later in life, the motive which should decide all that you do, must not be *your* gain. You must be concerned with the good of all.

If you find you are not in a position of an employer or supervisor, there is still one person whom you can and ought to rule. That is you! For only if you are master of yourself, are you ready to be the servant of others.

I pray for all.

Dr. J. H. Jowett, who was a great preacher at one time, used to tell of a girl who came to join his church. She was a servant, not well off, and not very well educated. He wanted to make sure that she knew what she was doing in taking vows of Christian church membership, so he asked her how she meant to live out her Christian life.

"I haven't much time off, sir," she said, "and I cannot attend many meetings or even many services."

"Well," said Jowett, "what will you do?"

"Well, sir," she said, "I always take the daily paper to bed with me at night."

Jowett was puzzled at this strange comment.

"What's the good of that?" he said.

"Well, sir," she said, "I look at the first page and I read the birth notices and I pray for the babies that have been born. Then I read the marriages and I pray that they may be happy and true. Then I read the deaths and I pray that God's comfort may come to these sorrowing homes."

I pray for all. Truly that girl did.
So can we all, every one of us.
Let's be sure we do it!

Read St. Luke 15: 3–10.

GOD'S CRUSADERS   Day Two

Let's look further at the motto from the Five Alls Inn.

I plead for all.
The writer of the letter to the Hebrews has a great vision, perhaps the greatest vision in the New Testament. He speaks of Jesus in heaven: "He ever liveth to make intercession for us" (Heb. 7: 25).
Even in heaven Jesus is pleading for men, that writer is saying. That is a remarkable picture of the concern and love of Jesus.

I fight for all.
The people who have loved humanity most have all done this. They saw a wrong, an iniquity, an oppression, some distress, some need. They fought to remove it.
Often they themselves were quite well-off and comfortable and lived in pleasant conditions. The winning of the struggle for social improvement was not going to profit them at all. Yet they were prepared to risk all for the sake of others.
I am sure you can think of people like this who have fought for the good of others—Albert Schweitzer, the great musician and medical missionary; Toyohito Kagawa, that

wonderful Japanese Christian; or, in our own times, Martin Luther King.

Too often we feel that, so long as things are well with us, we do not really care what is happening to others.

Great people take the sorrows of the world on their hearts, and become God's crusaders in the battle on behalf of those who are down-trodden and under-privileged and oppressed.

Read St. Matthew 15: 29–38.

WORK—FOR OTHERS!   Day Three

Here is one more thought that comes from the Five Alls Inn.

I work for all.
Do we?

One of the sad things in these days is that people don't work for each other. Some people work only for themselves, for a bigger bank balance, for a colour television set, a refrigerator, or a car. These are the things for which people do seem to work hard.

Some people do go a little further and work for their families, for a better chance for their sons and daughters, for a better start in life for them, a better job than they have. These are the things for which people do work.

Some people work for the group or party to which they belong, for more privileges, for higher pay, for shorter hours, for longer holidays, for better conditions for themselves and their mates.

These are the things for which people do work.

But there are so few, so very few, who work for *all*, who have a spirit of service which sees beyond the boundaries of self and selfish interest, who work for God and for all.

We must not work, as we grow up, only for ourselves.
We must work for all.

God so loved *the world*.
His love is for all.
We, who are his servants, must dedicate *our* lives to be
like him in this way.
We are responsible for *everyone* in need.

I hope that as you grow up you will truly work, not for
yourselves alone, nor only for your family and friends, but
for all.

Read St. Matthew 15: 21–28.

WHEN THE LIGHTS GO OUT   Day Four

I once stayed for a night at Banbury—the Banbury of the
famous rhyme "Ride a cock-horse to Banbury Cross".
Naturally I was interested to see the Cross, which the
nursery rhyme connects with the "fine lady on the white
horse".
But Banbury has also a very handsome church. I went
into it on the morning before I left, and there I saw something very wonderful.
As I came in through the front door, the church looked
very dark, for there was no lighting. Then I looked towards
the far end of the building. On the altar there was a polished
brass cross and that cross was shining like a star through
the dark. And what is more, there was no artificial lighting
on it.
With its own light that cross was shining so that it stood
out in the dark, even from far away.

J. L. Hodson, who was a famous journalist, tells in one
of his war-books of a conversation he had with a fellow

journalist on the morning after London's most devastating air-raid.

The journalist said to him, "Did you see the cross on St. Paul's, old boy? Nobody has ever seen it shine and glow as it did last night—as clouds of smoke rolled by it. It had an unearthly beauty all over it."

In the destruction and the devastation of that air-raid, the cross shone out.

I was once a parish minister in Renfrew on Clydeside in Scotland. I was visiting friends there in the days when Clydebank was devastated by air-raids in two terrible nights. My friends stayed in an avenue which was next door to the railway line.

Within sight of their house was a signal gantry, and the signal-lights formed exactly the shape of a cross.

I remember them saying to me, "So long as that cross of lights is lit, we know that there isn't going to be an air-raid. But when the lights are put out, we look for trouble."

The light of the Cross meant safety to my friends in Clydebank.

Read St. Luke 2: 27–33.

FOR WHOM THE LIGHT SHINES   Day Five

The light which shines from the Cross has always brought wonders in the dark. Let's just think of some of the things that have been done "in the name of the Cross".

It shone in the dark for the sick and the suffering and the weak.

Dr. A. Rendle Short wrote in *The Bible and Modern Medicine*, "We know from Jerome's writings that the first hospital of which we have any record . . . was founded by a Christian lady, Fabiola."

He goes on to tell us about the plague which smote

49

Carthage in A.D. 252. The heathen flung out their dead and fled.

But Cyprian, the Christian bishop, called the Christian congregation together and told them they must care for the sick and bury the dead. In doing this they would help to save the city from desolation.

Love, care and tenderness towards the sick, the infirm, the weak and the deformed were quite absent from heathen civilisation. But they shine from the Cross!

It shone in the dark for those who made moral mistakes.
The tragedy of the ancient world was not its lack of knowledge of the good. It was its inability to achieve it.

Seneca said that men both loved their vices and hated them. He complained bitterly at what he called "our inefficiency in necessary things".

People knew that they committed sins, but they felt helpless to do anything about it.

So St. Paul writes to the Corinthians, as he makes a list of their sins, and says that they are sinners, "And such were some of you" (1 Cor. 6: 9–11).

The Cross has always shown that it has to overcome sin and help the sinner to a happier life.

The light of the Cross shines for the sick and the sinner. Not all the darkness in the world can quench *that* light. This is the "good news" of the Gospel.

Read Colossians 1: 9–20.

THE SANCTUARY   Day Six

In London there is a little row of houses between West-minster Abbey and Dean's Court. Do you know its name? *I* think it is a lovely name.

Its name is *The Sanctuary*.

As I walked along The Sanctuary, I looked at some of the buildings of which it is composed. Suddenly I noticed that two of them stood out as insurance offices!

This seemed to me to be a parable of modern life. People seek their safety in earthly insurance. They seek a "sanctuary" in insuring themselves in terms of money.

I felt just a little bit sad, as I thought of that.

In one sense, of course, insuring oneself or one's possessions is not wrong. In fact it is good sense, for once a man has a wife and a family he has, in the old phrase, "given hostages to fortune". It would be unwise not to insure against the chances and changes of life. You must all do that.

But there is a way in which this linking of insurance and sanctuary is wrong.

Let's look at it this way.

In these days everybody is searching for security. But the real, live Christian has *never* sought security.

Think, for example, of the old days in the Roman Empire.

A man might say to a Christian preacher, "If I become a Christian, what may I expect?"

The honest answer would be, "You can expect imprisonment, crucifixion, the fight with the beasts in the arena, the stake and the flames. You will become an outlaw and your life will never be safe again."

Unamuno, who is a Spanish mystic, used to pray for those he loved, "May God deny you peace and give you glory."

Here again we are really thinking about the need to lose our lives to save them. Christians have always felt they mustn't put their own safety and security before the need to be obedient to Jesus.

And this feeling is right. Don't you think so, too?

Read St. John 16: 29–33.

I was sitting on a rock by the seaside, after I had parked the car.

Two little girls approached. They were about six or seven, and they were both pushing prams in which there were younger children.

One was another little girl of about three or four, and the other was a baby of about six or seven months.

The three-year-old was taken out of the straps in the pram, but the baby was left in his.

They played around for a bit, then one of them came up to me and said, "We're going along the shore and up another way, and back round by the sea-front. Will you look after the baby till we come back, mister?"

I said, "But what if he starts crying?"

"Oh," said the other little girl, "just lift him and walk about with him and sing to him." (Actually if I started singing to him, the baby was really going to have something to cry about!)

Off they went. Then I began to get worried. They were away so long that I began to think that they had either abandoned the baby, or forgotten about him, or got lost.

I began to get anxious about the time too. If I was going to get home at the right time, I had to leave soon. But I couldn't leave the baby!

I became more and more anxious, and more and more puzzled about what was going on and what to do. But I still felt that I couldn't go away and leave the baby, who fortunately had been quiet all the time. (Fortunately for him! I didn't need to sing to him!)

At last the little girls turned up again.

"Look," I said, "I thought you were lost. Aren't you frightened to go away and leave the baby like that?"

"Oh no, mister," said one of the little girls, "I knew you would take care of him."

Said the other, "I knew he would be all right with *you*!"

I was glad that I had waited, even if it had kept me late. I hadn't let down those little girls when they trusted *me*.

And I would hate to have done that.

It's so good to be trusted, isn't it?

Read St. Matthew 26: 20–25.

HE TRUSTS US Day Eight

We must never let down anyone who trusts us. This is worth thinking about a bit more.

This applies to God *for God has trusted us*.

That is why he has given us freedom. He could have made us like puppets on a string, doing whatever he laid down without any right to object. But then we would not have been free. God gave us "free will" so that we can obey or disobey him, accept or reject him, bring him joy or sorrow.

God puts *His* trust in *us*.

Our loved ones trust us, every day.

A husband trusts his wife, and a wife trusts her husband. You trust your parents completely and your parents trust you.

All the personal relationships you will make in life are founded on trust, as they must always be.

Jesus trusts us.

This is really what St. Paul meant when he spoke about the Church being the "body of Christ" (1 Cor. 12: 27; Eph. 1: 23). Jesus is no longer in this world as a human being, so if Jesus wants a task done, he has to get someone to do it for him.

That's where we come in. It seems strange, but this is what Jesus has done. He trusts *us* to work for him.

Christ has no hands but *our* hands to do His work today;
Christ has no feet but *our* feet to lead men on His way;
Christ has no lips but *our* lips to tell men that He died;
Christ has no help but *our* help to bring them to His side.

Read Revelation 3: 7–13.

PRAY AND WORK   Day Nine

There was once a man who had a large garden. It was very untidy, full of weeds and quite uncared-for, so he worked hard until it produced lovely flowers and very large vegetables.

A friend was being shown over the garden. He naturally commented on the beauty of the flowers and the excellence of the vegetables.

Then he said, "Yes, it's wonderful what God can do with a piece of ground, isn't it?"

"True," said the man who had worked so hard on the garden, "but you should have seen it when God had it to Himself!"

And that amusing little story says something that is very important.

It is what God and we do together that brings real blessing.

So it is a joint effort, always.

Work with God and he will work with and for you.

Read Exodus 3: 11–14.

LEARNING FROM THE UNLIKELY   Day Ten

I remember talking to a friend of mine who is a minister. I know him very well indeed, or thought I did. But he told me something which I had never suspected—that he had a very violent temper!

He also told me of a lesson that he had learned a long time ago. It was a lesson that had enabled him to control and master that temper.

At one time my friend had worked out in the East.

One morning, when he was shaving, his native servant came in and did something which annoyed him. He lost his temper with the poor man, took the soapy shaving-brush that he had in his hand and hurled it at the native boy. The brush missed its target and landed on the floor.

Without a word, the native boy stooped and picked up the brush and, with a courteous bow, handed it back to him.

My friend told me that that incident taught him a lesson which he never forgot.

Here he was, a so-called Christian, a member of a so-called more civilised race, losing his temper like that. Yet here was the boy, who was not a Christian at all, showing a perfect example of courtesy and forgiveness.

So my friend learned the lessons of courtesy and self-control from an Eastern native boy who was not a Christian at all.

And it influenced the rest of his life.

We all learn lessons from unlikely places in life.
I'm sure this will happen to you.
And you will be blessed by it.

Read St. Luke 7: 1–10.

UNLIKELY PLACES   Day Eleven

Let us just think of some unlikely people from whom we may learn lessons.

The Christian can often learn a lesson from the Communist.

A Communist knows what he believes. That is certain. He knows exactly what his creed is. He knows all it means and all it stands for. And he knows what demands it makes of him.

How many of us Christians know and understand our creed and our faith as well as the Communist knows and understands his?

That's one lesson we may learn from an unlikely person.

The Christian can often learn a lesson from the atheist.

The atheist often knows the Bible better than Christians do. If one is involved in an argument about what the Bible says, time and time again the atheist will be found to know the Bible in far greater detail than many religious people do. So, once again, we are taught a lesson in a most unlikely way.

Church people can often learn lessons from people like Jehovah's Witnesses.

Do you know what Jehovah's Witnesses are? They are people who call from door to door handing out literature and talking about their particular way of looking at religion. We don't always find Christians as willing to give time and effort for their faith as Jehovah's Witnesses are for their version of it. So, once again, we get a lesson from an unlikely source, don't we?

Read St. Luke 18: 9–14.

THE CLEVER MAN! Day Twelve

Jesus knew all about the sort of thing of which we were thinking yesterday. He told a story about it.

There was a steward, he said, who was a thorough-going rascal. In the old days, these stewards held most responsible positions. They had control of the whole estate. Often the master himself, even though he was rich, might not be able to read or write or count. So the steward had to look after everything for him.

This particular steward had used his position of trust to help himself to his master's money. But in due time he was found out. He began at once to "cook the books" as we say, to try to make the accounts look all right and arrange things so that the people who owed money would get away with much less than they really owed. He was going to see to it that, even when he was dismissed, he had friends who would feel they had to see him all right.

When the master found out about it, he appreciated the steward's cleverness! His steward might be a rascal, but he was very clever and he had to be admired! So Jesus finished up by saying, "The children of this world are in their generation wiser than the children of light" (Luke 16: 1-8).

What Jesus is really saying is this: "If religious people were half as much in earnest about their religion as business people are about their business, what a difference it would make!" If we were as keen about our faith as we are about the things we do for ourselves in life, we should be very active Christians!

If we would put effort into our Church as we put it into our ordinary work, what a difference it would make!

So, here again we learn lessons from unlikely places!

We learn from a clever rascal how we Christians ought to live!

That's a surprise, isn't it?

Read St. Luke 16: 1-8.

WORKING AND WAITING   **Day Thirteen**

The more I read of the lives of great men, the more I

57

recognise that they had the capacity to do two things. One was to work, and the other to wait.

I have mentioned Robert Southey before in *Marching Orders*, page 21. It was said of Southey that "he was never happy unless he was reading or writing a book." The capacity of great writers to work is extraordinary.

Perhaps the greatest example I know of a writer's industry is that of the famous novelist, Anthony Trollope.

Trollope was an inspector for the post office, first in Ireland and then in England. Because of the kind of work he did, he had to travel somewhere every day.

Trollope devised a certain kind of writing-pad which he could hold upon his knee, and, by his using this, the greater part of his early novels was written during journeys in railway trains!

On one occasion he had to go to Egypt on postal business. He describes the voyage, and says that not even its difficulties were allowed to interfere with his need to write.

"As I journeyed across France to Marseilles, and made thence a terribly rough voyage to Alexandria, I wrote my allotted number of pages every day," he writes. "On this occasion more than once I left my paper on the cabin table, but feeling very ill and having to go and lie down. It was February, and the weather was miserable, but still I did my work."

The ability to work is one of the marks of greatness.

So is the ability to wait. There is a time when we should just be quiet and at peace.

Strangely enough, Anthony Trollope himself tells us of Thomas Carlyle's reaction to his writing in trains. "Carlyle," says Trollope, "has since told me that a man travelling should not read, but 'sit still and label his thoughts'."

The famous Dr. Johnson used to say that one of the great uses of Sunday was that on it normal business was set aside, and it gave one the chance to sit quietly and to think about life.

Jesus said, "Come away by yourselves to a lonely place, and rest a while" (Mark 6: 31). The one who came to "work the works of him that sent me" (John 9: 4) knew the need to rest awhile.

To work and to wait: yes, these indeed are the things that make greatness possible.

Read Galatians 1: 11–24.

CALLING FOR HELP Day Fourteen

We once had a family motoring holiday. In ten days we covered no less than 1,467 miles!

We toured the north of Scotland. We went first to Fort William, then to Mallaig, to Inverness, and then, from there, we went right up to the far north, to Wick and to Thurso and to Bettyhill.

In doing that we travelled through some of the loneliest places in Scotland, and certainly over some of the most difficult roads.

As we travelled, I was struck by one thing. Wherever we went, even in the loneliest parts of the country, we would pass a telephone box. It might be in the middle of a moor, or on a lonely stretch of road, but all of a sudden, we would see one of these little red boxes ahead of us.

I found this a great comfort. It meant that no matter where you were, not very far away there was one of these little red telephone boxes, from which you could call for help.

Even in the most remote rural areas, if there was no telephone in a person's house, people could go, if there was illness or trouble, to one of these little red boxes and send a message for help.

And, what is more, you could do it twenty-four hours a day, at any time of the day, or at any time of the night, because there is always someone in the telephone exchange waiting to answer a call for help.

Abraham Lincoln, the famous President of the United States, spent a lot of time praying. Once one of his friends asked him how he could afford to waste—as he said—so much time in prayer. Lincoln answered, "I would be the greatest fool on earth, if I thought that I could sustain the demands of this high office without the help of a strength which is far greater than my own."

Just as there are the telephones that keep us in touch with help, so there is God to whom we can always call in our need.

And he is always there—day and night, all the time.

Read St. Luke 11: 1–4.

GOD IS THERE   Day Fifteen

One of the very famous generals of the First World War (1914–18) was the French general, Marshal Foch. He was in command of the allied armies in Europe and in this work carried a great responsibility.

On one occasion a staff meeting was called, and all the officers and commanders turned up but Foch himself did not appear.

One of his officers said, "I think I know where we can find him." He went round to a little ruined church near army headquarters and there, as he suspected, was Foch kneeling in prayer before the altar.

A great man like Foch knew that whenever he was in trouble and up against it, he could speak to God, and God would hear him.

We are never left alone.

God is always there to help.

60

The little red telephone boxes in the lonely parts of the country had another use.

If you lived somewhere in the wilds of those northern Scottish counties of Sutherlandshire, or Ross-shire, or Inverness-shire, you just wouldn't see your friends very often! To do that would be a day's journey!

When people who live in these remote parts of the country feel lonely and want to speak to their friends, all they need do is pick up that telephone and they can talk.

And that can be a great comfort.

Some time every day we should, as it were, "put a call through" to God. To keep in touch with him is our greatest joy and our greatest security.

Do it!

Read St. Luke 11: 5-13.

AN APPOINTMENT WITH GOD   Day Sixteen

There was at one time a well-known bishop called Bertram Pollock.

A bishop is a very busy man, with all kinds of meetings to attend and many calls on his time. But Bertram Pollock made it a rule to keep three periods in the day when he spoke to God.

On a certain day, just as one of these times was about to begin, a visitor came to the door. Bertram Pollock was told that a visitor had called. He said, "Put him in the side-room and tell him to wait for a minute or two. I've got an appointment with God."

It would be a good rule for us if we had a daily appointment with God. Then we can pray to him and tell him of our needs.

Prayer is our way of talking to him and of asking God

61

for help. Just as it is possible with telephone boxes, we can, as we said earlier, use prayer twenty-four hours a day, at any time in the day and the night, and God will be there to answer.

The Psalmist said, "This poor man cried, and the Lord heard him, and saved him out of all his troubles" (Psalm 34: 6).

No one ever put through a call to God which God did not hear.

So he will hear *you*.

Read Psalm 34: 1–6.

THANKS—FOR A MEMORY   Day Seventeen

I was born in Wick, which is a town right on the tip of north-east Scotland, which I had not seen since 1912—until I visited it recently. The extraordinary thing is that when I did go back, immediately and without any hesitation, I recognised the street where we used to live and I could go straight to the house where I was born!

Isn't memory a remarkable gift?

You will find as you grow up that there are many pictures that remain clearly on your mind for ever. The psychologists tell us that we never forget anything. That seems extraordinary, but in fact everything we have ever done or seen is registered somewhere in our minds, and all the things memory has stored up can affect us, *without our being aware that they are doing so.*

Obviously if we never forget anything, we should be very careful indeed what we give ourselves to remember!

What should we remember? How careful should we be? *We should be careful what we look at.*

62

Sir Joshua Reynolds, the great artist, would not look at an inferior painting. He said that even to look at an inferior picture had an effect on his own art, so he didn't do it!

Do you remember what I said about the influence of memory?

If we allow ourselves to look at soiled and unpleasant things, there is defilement in our memories, even if we are unaware that it is there.

Keep looking at whatever is good and lovely, and remember it!

And, of course, keep looking towards Jesus.

Read Philippians 4: 1–8.

LISTEN CAREFULLY! Day Eighteen

Remembering what we said yesterday about memory, *we should also be very careful what we listen to.*

An old man of whom I have been told said, "Almost fifty years ago I heard a profane joke and still remember it. How many pious passages of a far later date have I forgotten."

That man listened to something unpleasant, and it stayed in his memory. We should be very careful what we hear, for every questionable thing is going to remain in our memories.

Listen to that which is good and lovely and remember it.

And, of course, listen to Jesus.

We should also be careful what we read.

There is a strange but true story of the way in which a thing is never forgotten. It is the story of a certain servant girl.

She fell ill, and in her illness she suffered from delirium—she spoke without knowing what she was saying or doing.

In her delirium, she poured out a flood of language which

no one could understand. Then someone who knew the Hebrew language happened to be visiting her during one of her fits of delirium, and discovered that this servant girl was actually reciting whole chapters of the Old Testament in Hebrew!

She had never studied Hebrew, of course. But what had happened was this.

At one time she had been a serving-maid in a minister's house. The minister who lived there had been in the habit each morning of reading out loud to himself a chapter of the Hebrew Bible, as he walked up and down in his study. While he read, this girl had been sweeping and dusting and polishing the landing outside the study door.

She had heard this Hebrew, and, quite unknown to her, it had stayed in her memory. So in her fits of delirium, when she wasn't really in control of what she was saying, she remembered it and she recited it.

Read that which is good and lovely and remember it! And, of course, read about Jesus.

"Whatsoever things are true, whatsoever things are honest, whatsoever things are just, whatsoever things are pure, whatsoever things are lovely, whatsoever things are of good report; if there be any virtue, and if there be any praise, *think on these things*." (Philippians 4: 8).

Read 1 Corinthians 11: 23–28.

IT'S WORTH THE STRUGGLE! Day Nineteen

Do you like practising your music? I imagine it's a struggle sometimes!

Paderewski, one of the greatest pianists of all time, thought nothing of going over a bar of music as many as forty times until he was sure he was playing it exactly as it ought to be played.

Before a concert, he always played through the whole programme, though he had already played all of the pieces in that programme times without number.

One day Paderewski played before Queen Victoria, and the Queen was deeply moved by his performance.

"Mr. Paderewski," she said, "you are a genius."

"That may be," answered Paderewski, "but before I was a genius, I was a drudge."

There is nothing in this world worth learning that can be learned without a struggle. But this is what makes learning a thrill.

If something was easy to learn, there would be no kick in mastering it. The thrill is to struggle at it for a long time, then suddenly to have the excitement of discovering that one understands what did not before make sense.

Damon Runyon wrote to his son, "You will improve the more you write. Good writing is simply a matter of application, but I learned many years ago that the words will not put themselves down on paper in dreams or in conversations."

Writing is struggling to write—not dreaming about writing or talking about writing.

Learning the piano is struggling to practise, not dreaming about sitting playing in the Royal Festival Hall!

Growing in the Christian faith is not dreaming about haloes. It is trying hard to do better and be better for Jesus' sake.

But it's worth the struggle!

Read 2 Corinthians 4: 5–11.

65

Life is full of ups and downs! Whatever happens to you in life, I can promise you that in any day and in any week and all through life you will get the rough and the smooth, the sunshine and the shadow, the welcome and the unwelcome. Life is bound to be a mixture for you as it is for everyone else.

It is of great importance to remember that life is a *mixture*. You must therefore be ready to accept it as it comes.

In life there are going to be things you can do and things you cannot do.

Nobody in the world can do everything well. Each of us has abilities and each of us has weak points. It is a secret of successful living to realise what we can do, and do it, and to see our limitations and accept them.

You will come across people who pine for a job or a position that is just not for them and for which ability does not exist. That is a very unhappy experience.

One of the happiest experiences in life is to come across people who have realised both their capabilities and their limitations, and who have made the most of the talents they have.

Try to be the best you can be. Use all your gifts and talents. What you can't be or do, accept graciously!

In life there are pleasures we can have and pleasures we cannot have.

In every pleasure there is an element of danger. It is so easy for a pleasure to become an addiction, and for a habit to become our master. Pleasure is good. To think of nothing but pleasure is the way to unhappiness. For pleasure of itself can never satisfy.

Wise are those young people who realise the pleasures which are not for them!

Read 2 Corinthians 4: 13–18.

"COUNT YOUR BLESSINGS" Day Twenty-one

Let's take yesterday's thought a stage further.
There are things in life that we get and things that we do not get.

You will find two kinds of people in this world. There are the people who are always surprised that life has been so good to them. (They are usually not those who have the most!)

There are people in life who are always bitter and resentful because life has—*they feel*—kept so much back from them.

There are in fact a great many things which may not be for our good. Count the blessings you have which are good for you. As the old hymn says, it "will surprise you" how many blessings you have and have had—even at your stage of life!

Life is, as I said yesterday, a mixture. It is never made up of one colour. "Life like a dome of many coloured glass stains the white radiance of eternity," says one of our poets. Life is like a patchwork quilt, some light, some dark.

But have you noticed this about the colours in stained-glass windows and the colours in a patchwork quilt? Despite their diversity, they make a harmony.

Life can be like that for us all if we have learned to accept the mixture which is life and to make the best of it.

Life (as you will find) has the things we can do and the things we cannot do, the pleasures we can have and the pleasures we cannot have, the things we get and the things we do not get.

For those who love God it can still be a thing of harmony, for God always works things together for good to them that love him (Rom. 8: 28).

I hope your lives, as they develop, are *full* of blessings.

Read 2 Corinthians 6: 1–10.

I hope your lives, as they develop, are *full* of blessings.

Read 2 Corinthians 6: 1–10.

"COUNT YOUR BLESSINGS"

I am sure you like animals! Have you noticed how much the Old Testament prophets liked them too? It really is quite remarkable how much they said about them.

Take that famous passage in Isaiah for example.

In the dream of the future, the wolf and the lamb, the leopard and the kid, the calf and the young lion are to lie down in peace together.

And then there comes this lovely sentence: "They shall not hurt or destroy in all my holy mountain" (Isa. 11: 6–9).

The picture of what is sometimes called "the age of God" is of an age when all enmity, whether it is instinctive or produced in some other way, will be wiped out, and when there is a universal fellowship that takes in the whole creation.

If we are thinking of this only in relation to people, think of the fellowship of the twelve disciples.

In the Twelve there was *Matthew*, the tax-gatherer, the man who had sold himself into the service of his country's enemies to get rich quick, the traitor and the quisling. But there was also *Simon the Zealot*, who was a fanatical nationalist, and a man who was committed to try to clear the Romans out of Palestine. The methods would include violence and, if need be, murder and assassination. Simon came from that background.

There was a time, therefore, when Matthew and Simon the Zealot would have been the most deadly enemies, but in the company of Jesus, they found a fellowship that bridged their traditional quarrels.

Bryan Green, who is a well-known evangelist, tells of a campaign he held in America. After it, the converts were asked to say what the campaign had meant to them.

A negro girl spoke briefly because she was not used to speaking in public. This is what she said: "Through this campaign I have found Jesus and Jesus has enabled me to forgive the man who murdered my father."

So you see how Jesus reconciles us, not only to God, but to one another.

Read Isaiah 11: 1–9.

THE SILENT MINUTE — Day Twenty-three

Here is another part of our lives in which the need to be silent is real. *If we are to hear the voice of God, we should be quiet and listening.*

I think it is possible that we hear the voice of God so seldom because we listen for it so seldom! And by hearing the voice of God, I don't mean *literally* hearing a voice, but "hearing" it in our hearts. People sometimes feel God does not speak to them. But I ask them, "Do you ever give him the chance to speak to you?" If you talk all the time in a conversation with a friend, you certainly won't hear *his* views.

The Psalmist heard God say, "Be still and know that I am God" (Psalm 46: 10). He is right. It is in the quietness we hear God best. Elijah, you remember, found God not in the earthquake, the wind or the fire, but in a still, small voice (1 Kings 19).

There is a little book of prayers entitled *God's Minute.* A minute of listening in the morning and in the evening, at the day's beginning and at the day's ending, would make a world of difference to all our lives. It might be a good rule for you to keep a silent minute with and for God at the beginning and end of each day.

There are times when words are needed, when not to speak is to fail people *and* God. But, on the whole, it is

69

worth remembering that speech may do far more harm than silence.

It is harder for all of us to learn *not* to speak than to learn to speak!

Read St. Luke 9: 18–24.

A STORY OF HOPE   Day Twenty-four

O. Henry is the name of a very famous writer of short stories. One of these is about a boy who was brought up in a country town.

He had once been a good boy, but he moved to a large city and there he got involved with bad company. He learned to do wrong, but to do it very successfully!

He became a skilled pickpocket and a thief. He had never been caught, and he was very pleased with himself about that. He was, as it were, at the top of his profession!

One day he was going down a city street. He had just stolen a wallet and snatched a bag, and made himself a large "profit".

All of a sudden he saw a girl about his own age. He looked again, and he recognised her. She used to sit beside him in the same class in the village school in the old days when he had been good and innocent.

When he looked at her, he could see that she was still the same lovely girl as she had always been.

She didn't see him. But the very sight of her made him look at himself. He immediately saw himself as the petty sneak-thief that he was.

He leaned his forehead against the cool iron of a lamppost. "O God, how I hate myself," he said.

I find that story sad, but encouraging. The boy who had taken the wrong way was still able to see good, to recognise the good and to feel very sad over his own failure.

70

So I see this as a story with hope in it.
That, I find, feels good.

Read St. Luke 15: 11–32.

GOD'S GIRL ... OR BOY Day Twenty-five

During the Second World War, I had something to do with a canteen which was run for the troops in the town in which I was then working. Early on in the War we had billeted, in our town, a number of Polish troops who had escaped from Poland.

Among them there was a Polish airman. When we could persuade him to talk, he would tell the story of a series of hair-breadth escapes.

He would tell us how somehow he had escaped from Poland, how somehow he had made his way across Europe, how somehow he had crossed the Channel, how somehow he had been shot down in his aeroplane once, and crashed on another occasion.

But what impressed me was this, he always ended the story of his escapes from death with the same words: "I am God's man."

Here was a man who truly felt that God had dealt wonderfully with him and that in some way he belonged from then on to God, and had a special duty to Him.

The great Scottish preacher, W. M. McGregor, used to have a favourite way of beginning his prayers: "Thou hast made us and we are Thine; Thou hast redeemed us and we are doubly Thine."

This is what Paul meant when he said, "Do you not know . . . you are not your own? For you are bought with a price" (1 Cor. 6: 19, 20).

Every one of us is really God's man, woman, boy, girl.
And we have to live in his way because of that.

Read 1 Corinthians 6: 19–20.

Mark Rutherford wrote a novel in which he describes the marriage of a woman who had lost her first husband to another woman. She had a teenage daughter, but the second husband could make nothing of the girl. She seemed sullen and unhappy. There was nothing about her that seemed good and nice.

Then one day her mother fell ill. Immediately that girl changed completely. She became the perfect nurse. There was a new happiness about her. Nothing was a trouble. No service was too difficult for her to render. She did everything she could.

So a girl who had seemed very unpleasant turned out to be an excellent girl.

Isn't that strange?

They say that there is a certain kind of mineral that when you take it first in your hand, it looks like a dull and lustreless piece of stone. It has no life, no sparkle, no brilliance. But if you keep turning it over, you will, in the end, get it into a certain position when the rays of light strike it in a certain way, and it will begin to shine and sparkle like a diamond!

The sparkle is there if you will only look for it long enough.

People are like this. Everyone does something well. Everyone has some redeeming feature. Everything is beautiful . . . as a modern poem says. And everyone. But it sometimes takes a long time to see it!

Wouldn't it be wonderful if we could see that lovely side in our friends and especially in the people or playmates we don't like?

So let's always keep looking for that good part of some-one. If we can just have patience, we may get some very pleasant surprises!

Read St. Luke 19: 1–10.

Jesus was someone who was able to see the good side of people. Who could have thought that an impetuous soul like Peter, or a pair of arguers like James and John with a nickname like "sons of thunder", could be the foundation of the Christian church? But Jesus saw their value.

Not many people would have picked a pessimist like Thomas to be a right-hand man, would they? But Jesus saw his real nature and value.

Not many people would have wanted to pay a visit to a tax-gatherer like Zacchaeus or to have had a traitor like Matthew among his closest friends. But Jesus did. He knew the good side of these men.

Yes, Jesus had the ability to see the real strength and beauty in every life, and to find the hero in every man. He can see the potential hero or heroine in *you*!

Wouldn't life be happier if we were able to look below the surface and see the good in others?

If you try to do that, I'm sure you will often make new friends in very unexpected places!

Read St. John 4: 5–15.

REACH OUT!   Day Twenty-eight

I remember reading in a book about a game two children used to play.

One said to the other, "When you are going along the road, do you ever pretend that there is something terrific waiting for you round the next corner, and you've got to go and face it? It makes walking so exciting."

Yes, the unexpected is exciting!

Jesus told a story about a man who found a tremendous

treasure in a field (Matt. 13: 44). That man must have been ploughing or digging or weeding that field, and it was in the ordinary day's work that he found the treasure.

Every day brings opportunities—the opportunity to be a hero or a heroine in a way that really matters. It is the heroism of carrying on when we are up against it. To learn how to get up and fight on is a lesson worth learning: to think not of ourselves, but of others. This is the greatest of all honours, the honour of serving and helping someone in need.

Emily Dickinson has a lovely and simple little poem:

If I can stop one heart from breaking
 I shall not live in vain;
If I can ease one life the aching,
 Or cool one pain,
Or help one fainting robin
 Into his nest again
I shall not live in vain.

"If I can help somebody, as I pass along," says the song, "then my living will not be in vain."

That is true. The secret of life is in finding that helping others is much better than worrying about ourselves!

Don't be self-centred!
Reach out to others!

Read St. Matthew 13: 44–46.

LAUGH ... AND GROW FIT!   **Day Twenty-nine**

The doctors tell us that it is a literal medical fact that he who laughs most lives longest, for laughter expands the lungs and makes a man breathe deeply.

It is good to laugh as we said at the beginning of this

book. It was the philosopher, Thomas Hobbes, who said, "Laughter is nothing else but sudden glory."

It was that lovable musician, Haydn, who said, "God will forgive me, if I serve him cheerfully."

It is strange how often Christians have not always encouraged laughter. Sometimes Christian people seem afraid to laugh!

Eric Linklater tells of a school report he received when he was a schoolboy: "On the whole he is doing fairly well, but he is handicapped by a sense of humour."

Jesus could teach with a smile. What a picture he drew when he talked about the man with a plank in his own eye trying to remove the speck of dust from some one else's eye! (Matt. 7: 3–5). Can you imagine that?

How the disciples must have loved it when the nickname "sons of thunder" was attached to that tempestuous pair James and John! They really were "sons of thunder"!

Laugh a lot. It will help to keep you fit.
It is also a Christian thing to do.
What is more, it will help *you* a lot.
And *others* too!

Read St. Luke 6: 20–21.

THE FIRST STEP   Day Thirty

There is a story which tells how a crowd was watching an accident which had happened to a carter and which had wrecked his cart.

Amongst them there was an old Quaker.

Many were the expressions of sympathy for the carter in his loss.

Amid all the words, the old Quaker stepped forward. "I

75

am sorry five pounds," he said, handing a note to the carter.

Then he turned to the crowd. "Friends," he said to each, "how much art thou sorry?"

It is good to express sympathy in words.
It is much, much better to put it into practical help!
Don't you agree?

The Christian should never be behind in forgiveness.

We should always be ready to try to right wrongs or make friends with those with whom we have quarrelled. Even if we feel that we have been wronged and insulted; even if we feel, and feel rightly, that the fault is on the other side, we as Christians should always be ready to take the first step towards "reconciliation". It is the Christian's duty to heal division.

Many and many a quarrel and a bitterness would long since have been put right if only someone had been willing to take the first step towards ending them.

It is this first step which is so important in "quarrel-mending".

Let's try to be "first-step" people all through our lives!

Read St. Matthew 18: 21–35.

NO STATUS SYMBOLS   Day Thirty-one

"A man's life," Jesus said, "does not consist in the abundance of his possessions" (Luke 12: 15).

We cannot make what we can get in life the real test of things.

It's not money or position that is of real value: it is the kind of boy or girl you are and the man or woman you will become.

Again and again the Bible insists that, as the Authorised

Version has it, there is no "respect of persons", or, as the RSV has it, "no partiality" with God (Acts 10: 34; Rom. 2: 11). Status symbols and class distinctions mean nothing to God.

A pedigree is an odd thing. (Dogs have pedigrees, don't they? But sometimes people think they have them too!) The only difference between people is that some know their pedigree and some do not.

In 1783 the then Duke of Norfolk planned to invite to a family party all the living descendants of the first Duke who was killed at Bosworth in 1485.

When he had traced more than 6,000, he abandoned it as hopeless.

In 1911, it was calculated that the number of Edward the Third's descendants still living numbered somewhere between 80,000 and 100,000. But in the end all our pedigrees go back to the beginning! We all come from the same stock. Or, as we say in Scotland, "We're a' Jock Tamson's bairns."

We are.
God is not interested in pedigrees.
He is only interested in *us*.

Read Romans 2: 11–16.

MONTH THREE

How many parts are there in a typewriter? I don't know, but I have been told it is well over two thousand!

So it must take hundreds of people to make a typewriter!

When I thought of that, I began to think of the hundreds and hundreds of people whose names I do not know and will never know, but who helped me to write this book for you! *I* couldn't do my work without a typewriter. *I* couldn't have a typewriter without the work of hundreds of people. So, as I type, I can't help thinking of my army of nameless helpers.

We are all so dependent—and in so many ways—on an army of helpers whose names we shall never know.

Think of this for example.

I wonder how many hundreds of people, from how many different countries, are needed to produce *one* breakfast.

There is the farmer and his workers who grow the grain from which the bread is made.

There are the people in India or China or Ceylon who grew the tea from which the tea is made.

There are those who helped to provide the milk, the bacon, the eggs, the oranges for the marmalade. There are the sailors who carried some of our food across the sea, the transport workers who brought it along the roads and the railways, the people in the factories who helped to manufacture it, the shopkeepers who sold it.

The list of people who help us to have breakfast each morning is endless!

I never cease to be moved and thrilled by the thought of this army of people. Our dependence on that "nameless multitude" is an amazing thing.

"I am a debtor (under obligation) to others," said Paul (Rom. 1: 14).

"We are members one of another," he said, too (Rom. 12: 5).

Just as the body cannot do without its many parts, so we cannot do without each other.

There is a strange but vivid phrase in the Old Testament which speaks of being "bound up in the bundle of life" (1 Sam. 25: 29). It is saying the same thing.

We are all dependent on the nameless host of helpers.

So we ought to be very thankful people.

Read 1 Corinthians 12: 4–11.

CONTINUING STORY   Day Two

The "gauge" of railway lines in Britain, (that is the distance between the lines) is 4 feet $8\frac{1}{2}$ inches. The old Great Western Railway tried to break away from this. It used a 7 foot gauge, but in the end, in spite of the efforts of Brunel, its great engineer, it was compelled to fall in with the standard size.

4 feet $8\frac{1}{2}$ inches seems a very odd distance indeed.

How did it come about?

There is more than one explanation of it, but I have come across this interesting one.

The first railway-lines were laid for carts, to be hauled over by horses. A horse could haul a much heavier load if the cart or waggon ran on rails rather than on a road. The first rails were therefore laid on wooden boards which had themselves been laid on the top of the ruts which waggon- and cart-wheels had already made on the roads. The rails were laid to fit the ruts which were already there!

But here is the next question! Why were the cart ruts 4 feet $8\frac{1}{2}$ inches in gauge?

To explain this, a very ingenious suggestion has been made: that the distance between the wheels of a Roman chariot was 4 feet $8\frac{1}{2}$ inches. That's really what started the whole thing!

Centuries ago Roman chariots left their ruts on the roads; carts and waggons were built to the same gauge; and then, later on, the rails were laid to that gauge too.

If all this is true, *there was a direct connection between the Roman chariot and the Flying Scotsman thundering to London at a hundred miles an hour.*

This is true in other ways. There is a direct link between the first coracle to float on the water (like those St. Columba used to reach Iona) and the Cunarder *Queens* that, not so many years ago, crossed the Atlantic.

There is a direct connection between the first tree trunk that was flung across a stream to make a bridge and the newest modern bridge.

It is all a continuing story!

Read Genesis 3: 1–6.

OUR DEBT TO THE PAST   Day Three

Let us think about that "continuing story" of the railway lines.

Here is the first lesson.

The present grows out of the past. We are linked to what happened in the past, just as people in the future will have links with us.

What we do now will affect things in years to come.

The Church is one of the greatest examples of this. It began so long ago and we enjoy being part of it today.

Truly a "continuing story" in which God has been guiding events.

Jesus said this very thing about his disciples. "Others have laboured," he said, "and you have entered into their labour" (John 4: 38).

Each generation is like a link in a great chain. We are

linked to what has gone before and, of course, to what is going to come after us.

So we have to think a great deal about what *we* do. It will help—or harm—others in the future.

This, too, we should remember. We owe a lot to the past. We gain and benefit so much from what others have done.

We should always be grateful for those who have gone before us.

Read 1 Corinthians 3: 1–9.

OPPORTUNITY KNOCKS   Day Four

Do you remember these two parables that stand together in the thirteenth chapter of St. Matthew's Gospel? They are the parables of the treasure hidden in a field and that of the pearl of great price.

Here are four thoughts that these parables put before us. *These stories are about men who were able to grasp an opportunity.*
The ability to see an opportunity is a great asset.

Do you know about the army commander who, when he realised his army was ambushed, said to his general, "We have fallen into the hands of the enemy"?
The general immediately answered, "No, why not say that they have fallen into our hands?"

Or do you remember these lines?

> Two men looked out through prison bars;
> One saw mud, the other saw stars.

It all depends how you see the situation—as a crisis or an opportunity.

The Christian way is to grasp that opportunity and every opportunity, just as did the men who found the treasure and the pearl of great price.

Read Proverbs 2: 1-5.

GRASP THAT OPPORTUNITY! Day Five

We are going to look further at these two parables we considered yesterday—the parables of the treasure and the pearl.

We thought first, didn't we, about the way that, in both cases, the opportunity had been grasped. Now let us note how immediately the decision to grasp the opportunity was taken.

Have you seen that ancient—or as we sometimes say "classic" picture of Opportunity? She (and she is seen as female!) has lots of hair in front and none at the back. So long as you grasp her when she is approaching you, you are all right! But fail to take that chance, and Opportunity has gone. If she passes you, you can't grab her and pull her back. There is nothing to grasp!

There is an old proverb that says, "There are three things that never come back—the spent arrow, the spoken word, and the lost opportunity."

It's true!

In both stories, the people involved were prepared to pay the price of the opportunity. They sold all they had to get the field and the pearl. They were happy to bear the cost of turning opportunity into reality. They were ready when opportunity knocked.

There are sometimes people who just won't pay the price . . . like the rich young ruler in the New Testament. Jesus had to let him go away—and he felt sorry to see him go, because he liked him—because he could not give up his possessions.

Count the cost!
If it's worth it, you will want to pay it!

Read St. Matthew 19: 16–22.

THE GOLFER   Day Six

There are two golf courses where we usually spend our holidays. One is a good course. You could play a championship on it. The other is a course for children, older people and the inefficient.
I play on the second!

What I like about this second course is that it hasn't got an inch of "rough" (i.e. thick grass) on it anywhere. Everywhere the grass is short and smooth, so you stand on the tee and you hit the ball as far as you can. But if you "slice" the ball (as golfers say) or "pull" it, you don't need to worry. It will be lying in the nice, short, green grass, and you will have no difficulty in finding it or playing it.
So you usually manage to "hole out" (as golfers say) in four shots or possibly five. And you think you're pretty good!

Well, I played all through my holiday on the course with no rough on it, where I could hit the ball as hard as I could, without worrying where it landed. So I said to myself when it was time to go home, "I'm not so bad yet. I can *still* play!"
But soon after we came home from holiday, I had a job to do in a town where there are some first-class golf courses. I decided to take my clubs with me and to have a game after my work was done.
I hadn't played three holes when I discovered that on a

real course, where there was a "fairway" flanked by two stretches of deep rough, you just couldn't slice or pull the ball two hundred yards without getting into very serious trouble. So if you weren't aiming straight, you were in trouble all the time.

I wasn't aiming straight. So, as a golfer, I was found out!

You will find that this is true in life too, if you think about it.

Read 2 Timothy 4: 1–8.

THE HARD WAY   Day Seven

Things should never be made too easy for us. This I learned from my golf experiences! If things are made too easy, we are just not ready to face real tests when they come.

This is one reason why the standards of your school or club should be as high as they can be. And the same is true of belonging to a church. Make things too easy and there is trouble ahead.

It is never wise to encourage the idea that we can make mistakes and escape punishment.

My too easy golf-course made me forget that, on a real course, mistakes *are* punished. I had to learn all over again that you just can't make mistakes and "get away" with them.

So if you think your master is strict and drives you too hard, perhaps it's because he knows this is true. He wants you to learn. If you learn "the hard way", you will have learned well!

We must all be on our guard against wanting things which are too easy, or wanting things made too easy. As the Bible says, "Blessed is the man whom thou dost chasten, O Lord" (Psalm 94: 12).

Or again, "The Lord disciplines him whom he loves" (Heb. 12: 6).

God sometimes has to make us learn the hard way.

Read St. Matthew 7: 13–14.

A LETTER FROM AMERICA   Day Eight

The postman brought a letter from America. It was from a man who had read one of my books, and had noticed my name.

He wrote to ask if, by any chance, I was the son of a W. D. Barclay of Motherwell in Lanarkshire, Scotland, who had been a bank manager in Motherwell, and was also a local preacher there.

I am! We lived in Motherwell when I was a boy. My father was a banker by profession, but at heart he was a preacher. His name was known as a preacher all over Lanarkshire!

It is twenty-five years since he died, but there are many places in Lanarkshire, but also all over Scotland, where I am still my father's son!

To few boys—or girls for that matter—can there ever have been given as good a father and mother as I was given.

"Let us now praise famous men," sang the Son of Sirach, "and the fathers that begat us" (Eccl. 44: 1 in the *Apocrypha*). Indeed we should do this!

Heine, the German philosopher, once said that a man could not be too careful in the choice of his parents!

There are few greater blessings in this world than the gift of good parents.

We don't choose them, but, when God has blessed us with them, he has given us a gift for which we can never be grateful enough.

G. K. Chesterton used to tell how, when he was a boy,

88

he had a toy theatre with cardboard characters. One of the characters was the figure of a man with a golden key. He had long since forgotten what character the cardboard figure actually stood for, but he always connected the man with the golden key with his father. His father, he said, unlocked all kinds of wonderful things to him.

Fathers and mothers do wonderful things for us.

Be grateful for your parents.

Read Exodus 20: 1–17.

COLD WATER

You know the phrase about "pouring cold water" over a suggestion or a plan. It means you don't think it will work, so you discourage it.

But sometimes "pouring cold water" on things can become a habit! And a bad habit, I should say!

In the Royal Navy, "cold water" is forbidden! It is a Navy regulation that no officer shall speak "discouragingly" to any other officer.

That's excellent!

It should be like this in the Church. But you don't always find encouragement there.

A certain American said, "No man has a right so to preach as to send his hearers away on flat tyres. Every discouraging sermon is a bad sermon ... a discouraged person is not an asset but a liability."

And think sadly of this comment from Robert Louis Stevenson's diary: "I have been to church today and am not depressed." It was so unusual for him not to be depressed by church!

So don't be a "cold-water pourer"!
It is so easy to discourage.
What we really need is encouragement.
And God's servants should certainly be able to give that.

Read Acts 3: 1–10.

ENCOURAGEMENT   Day Ten

Here is another form of "pouring cold water".
There are those who hit a man when he is down.

When I was a boy I played cricket. There was one season
when nothing would go right.

But I am not alone in that! Even the great Don Bradman
could fail. J. M. Barrie once said in one of his cricket
speeches, "The first time I saw Bradman bat, he made one;
the next time I saw him he was not so successful."

I had had three successive weeks when I was not so
successful, and I was feeling very discouraged. The next
week I was surprised to see my name on the team list at all,
because I had expected to be dropped.

The afternoon of the game came and the "batting order"
was put up. I went to look at it, expecting to see myself low
down in the batting order in the "tail" of the team—as my
series of "ducks" deserved. Lo and behold, I discovered
from the list that my captain had moved me up to open the
innings.

He was a *very* wise man, that captain! I squared my
shoulders, went out and made up for at least some of the
noughts.

It was encouragement that did it.

When someone has been a failure, that is the very time,
not to discourage, but to *encourage* him.

"Be of good cheer," said Jesus (John 16: 33).
He encourages *us*.
We must encourage *others*!

Read 2 Kings 2: 9–14.

HOW ACCIDENTS HAPPEN   Day Eleven

How do accidents happen?
I began to drive a car in 1933—over forty years ago! I
thought it might be a good idea if I looked back over that
period and saw if I could work out the answer to that
question.
My first answer is *impatience* and *irritation*!
Someone wants to pass us, but we do not want to be
passed, so we do what we can to prevent that happening.
Or we get behind a slow-moving vehicle and lose patience.
So we take a risk. We try to pass when we shouldn't and
an accident happens.
An irritated driver is a bad driver.

This incidentally is true of life too. There is nothing that
clouds our judgment as impatience and irritation do.
Three times Psalm 37 (verses 1, 7, 8) gives us the advice:
"Fret not yourself." "Fret not yourself," it says, "it tends
only to evil."
Don't ever lose your temper!

Accidents happen, too, when people just won't concentrate. There can hardly be a driver in this world who has
not found himself in real trouble because his attention
wandered for a split second. But when you think of the
speed of the modern car, not even a split second of inatten-
tion or lack of concentration is safe.

This is true of life too. It is the careless moment that
brings life to shame or even to ruin.

The New Testament says "Watch!" (Matt. 24: 42).
If you don't "watch" what you are doing all the time, there is trouble ahead.

Concentrate!

Read St. Matthew 24: 42–51.

"IT WON'T HAPPEN . . ." Day Twelve

Here is another cause of car accidents.
A driver wants, as we say, "to show off". Perhaps he wants to impress his passenger. He takes risks.
But in the end he takes a risk once too often.
"It can't happen to me," he says.
But it does.

Life works in just the same way.
"It can't happen to me," we say.
But it does.
"Pride goes before destruction," says Proverbs 16: 18. It does.
That drink, for example. "It won't harm *me*," we say.
Those drugs, for example. "*I* can take them all right," we say.
But we take risks when we have such false confidence and false pride.
We could end in trouble!

Being clever is really a dangerous game.
Of course, when we are young, we think we know best. We're not willing to listen to the advice of older people.
But sometimes the voice of experience should be heard. For it may be the voice of someone who also thought *he* could risk it.
But he couldn't.

Whether on the road—on foot or bicycle—or on the road of life, don't take too many risks.

You can get yourself into a lot of trouble.

Read Proverbs 16: 16–22.

SMILERS Day Thirteen

Joy is one of the commonest New Testament words.

Dr. Russell Maltby, who was a famous Christian writer, once said, "Jesus promised his followers three things:

"They would always be in trouble!

"They would be quite fearless!

"They would be absurdly happy!"

So, if you are a Christian, you should be happy and joyful!

This doesn't always happen, I'm afraid.

It was said of the famous Scottish poet, Robert Burns, that he was "haunted" rather than "helped" by his religion. In other words, he was made afraid by his religion, when he ought to have been made happy by it.

There are far too many people who think religion is dark clothes and gloomy faces. Jesus found some of the Pharisees were like that.

You remember how he said, "Don't be like the 'hypocrites'" (that really means "play-actors" or "pretenders") and be "of a sad countenance". Christianity isn't like that. It's a religion of joy.

You are going to enjoy life if you are a Christian! It's the right thing to do. So be a smiling, happy Christian.

You will help many other people if you do.

And you will be much more like the kind of boy or girl Jesus can use.

He needs smiling followers! Smilers, in fact!
Be happy.

Read St. Luke 6: 27–35.

MY BROTHER'S KEEPER   Day Fourteen

"Aeroplane crashes in Siberia."
"Thousands die of hunger in Pakistan."
"Children murdered in Hong Kong."

Do you read reports like these in your newspapers?
I find I don't. If it is "aeroplane crash in southern
England"—that's a different story. Then I'm interested.
If it's "Family dies of hunger in Birmingham" (or
Glasgow or Dublin), I'm interested.
If it's "Child murdered in London", I look and read
further.

When it's near and involves my fellow countrymen, I am
concerned.
When it's far away and involves a different nation, I don't
care so much.
Yet in both cases people suffer.
And in both cases, the people who are harmed matter to
God.

I don't feel very happy about my failure in this matter.
And I would rather you didn't make the same mistake, and
be as thoughtless as I feel I am.
Broken hearts are broken hearts anywhere.
Starvation is always awful suffering, wherever it happens.
Trouble is trouble whoever is involved.

Cain said to God when he was questioned about his
brother Abel's murder, "Am I my brother's keeper?"

The answer is "Yes, of course I am."
And my brother is *anyone, anywhere.*

Read 1 John 5: 13–20.

SOMEBODY LOVES YOU!   Day Fifteen

Aren't people funny? I mean "funny" in this sense that they do what seem to us such strange things!

And this has always been true. Here are some very curious people:

"An old wife of Attica, so they say," reports the ancient writer Sextus Empiricus, "swallowed thirty drams of hemlock and took no harm, and Lysis took four drams of poppy juice and was none the worse for it."

"Demophon, Alexander's butler, used to shiver when he was in the sun or in a hot bath, but felt warm in the shade."

"Athenagoras the Argive took no hurt from the stings of scorpions or poisonous spiders."

And here are some more funny people from those olden times:

"Rufinus of Chalcis drank hellebore like someone drinking a cup of lemonade."

"Andron the Argive was never thirsty, not even when crossing a desert, and never drank water."

"Tiberius Caesar could see in the dark."

So Sextus Empiricus gives us his extraordinary list of people who liked unpleasant and even poisonous things.

I have known people who loved undiluted lemon juice in all its bitterness, and who actually enjoyed drinking castor oil! That seems funny to me!

Yet to someone, everyone, however odd to us, is important. Somebody loves him.

This makes me feel better! Even though I am a strange person with funny ways, my wife and children still love me.

And the same is true for *you*. Even though you have funny ways, you are still loved!

"Love is blind," is an ancient saying. It is, but it is good!

Love does not see our faults and our failings. Love is still ours. Somebody loves you!

If there is no one on earth to love us, it is still true that God loves us.

During the First World War King George V and Queen Mary, one Christmas, sent Christmas cards to all the soldiers in the army.

There was a soldier who had no friends and no relations; he was alone in the world. He had received nothing at Christmas. Then the royal Christmas card came.

"Even if no one else remembers me," he said, "my king and queen do."

One of the Psalms says, "For my father and mother have forsaken me, but the Lord will take me up" (Psalm 27: 10).

Somebody loves you!

Read Psalm 27.

HELLO, BROTHER!   **Day Sixteen**

Do you remember how Ananias addressed St. Paul when he met him for the first time?

"Brother Saul," he said (Acts 9: 17).

Think about this.

You remember how St. Paul (who was called Saul of Tarsus before he became St. Paul) had persecuted Christians wherever he found them. His reputation was known far and wide for this. And he had actually set off for Damascus to do just this!

96

Thus it was, you remember, that he was "converted" on the road to Damascus. Jesus seemed to come to him and ask him why he was treating Christians like that. The story is told in Acts, chapter 9.

Ananias was the first person St. Paul met after his dramatic experience.

Now Ananias knew his reputation, knew (as it says in the first verse of that chapter) that St. Paul (who was, as I say, then "Saul of Tarsus") had been "breathing murderous threats" against Christians. Yet here he was, with no hint of suspicion or anger, and without any hesitation, greeting him as "Brother Saul".

To be able to offer a hand in friendship in these circumstances was one of the most wonderful actions in the Bible.

If we could have the spirit of Ananias, we would all be wonderful people.

Read Acts 9: 10–22.

ENABLERS   Day Seventeen

Let's think a little bit more about the remarkable attitude of Ananias to "Brother Saul".

Ananias might well have said, "Even if this Saul is converted, we want nothing to do with him in Damascus. He'll have to show a lot of changes before *we* accept him."

But Ananias did the better thing.

He forgave and he forgot.

It is not easy to forgive things people have done to you. It is even harder to forget them.

I have known people who have remembered things people have done long years after it all happened.

There were two elderly ladies who attended an East End

city church. They sang and prayed and thought together in the same congregation. They took the Lord's Supper together. But in twenty-five years they had not spoken to each other because of a quarrel away in the past.

This is unbelievable, isn't it? But it happens.
That is how not to behave.
Follow Ananias's way!

This too we should remember.
Ananias, by what he did, brought someone far greater than himself into the Church.
We can all help Jesus's work by being helpers—or "enablers"—in this way.
Like Andrew, we can introduce someone to Jesus!
Peter was important but so was Andrew, the enabler!
Enable!

Read St. John 12: 20–22.

THE GO-BETWEEN   Day Eighteen

Have you heard of Tychicus?
Tychicus is mentioned four times in the Letters of Paul in Ephesians 6: 21; Colossians 4: 7; 2 Timothy 4: 12; Titus 3: 12. On every one of these occasions, Paul is sending him somewhere with a letter or with a message!
Tychicus was one of Paul's most trusted "go-betweens". Tychicus never speaks or writes in his own name. He is always speaking and writing *in the name of Paul*. He is the middleman.

"Go-betweens" are important people.

We need the go-between where people are concerned.
In the New Testament one of the basic meanings of the

word *peace* is "right relations between one person and another". To create a right relationship between two people, especially if they have had a dispute, was, according to the Rabbis, one of the greatest things that anyone could do. To be a reconciler, a "go-between", was something to bring joy in this world and honour in the life to come.

Jesus said: "Blessed are the peacemakers" (Matt. 5: 9). So I add, "Blessed are the go-betweens", for they bring people together.

There are people who go about doing things and saying things that create divisions between people. They are doing the devil's work!

There are people who try always to bring people together. They are doing Jesus's work!

We need a go-between so far as God and man are concerned. We need someone to bridge the gap that seems to exist between God and man.

We have that person in Jesus. He is the middleman, the go-between.

Mesos is the Greek for "in the middle". A *mesites* was one who stood in the middle, and who brought two separated people together. This is just what Jesus does with us and God. He is the *mesites*.

That is why Jesus is often called the "Mediator".

That means, really, the go-between.

Read Hebrews 10: 19–22.

HOBSON'S CHOICE   Day Nineteen

Have you heard the phrase "Hobson's Choice"?
I have by chance discovered its origin.

In Cambridge the name Hobson keeps appearing.
There is a *Hobson Street*.
There is a *Hobson's Conduit*, which used to stand in the

99

centre of the Market Place and which is now in Trumpington Street.

For a Mr. Hobson kept a livery stable in Cambridge in the seventeenth century.

If you came to him to hire a horse, it was his rule that you took the one next to the door. If you wouldn't take that one, you got none at all!

It is from this Hobson and his insistence that you took the horse next to the door, and no other, that there comes the phrase *Hobson's Choice*.

So to be faced with Hobson's Choice means simply that you have no alternative. You must accept what is there!

You may sometimes be faced with Hobson's Choice in life. Illness has sometimes left people with no choice as to the kind of work that they can do. Misfortune and lack of money may have left people with no choice as to what they can possess.

Disappointment leaves us with no choice as to what we must go on doing. What others do sometimes closes doors that might have been open to us.

In such a situation, and in life, everyone meets this—the great secret and the great virtue is to accept what we have and to get on with the job.

There are too many adults, who, because they did not get what they wanted, have become soured, embittered, quarrelsome and sometimes even obstructive towards those who have received what was denied to themselves.

The Stoics, that famous Greek group of philosophers of olden times, had a saying. It sounds merciless but it is true!

"If you can't get what you want, want what you can get."

It is really quite a good rule for life.

Read Paslm 125.

100

Martin Luther, the great Protestant reformer, faced a Hobson's Choice when he stood out against things he felt were wrong in the Church of his time.

Listen to what he says:

"Here I stand. I can do no other, so help me, God."

Luther felt he faced Hobson's Choice on principle. It wasn't that he was not free to give up the fight. He could have done that. But no! He felt "principles" were involved. He had a moral duty to carry on his cause, whatever the cost.

There is a phrase that says, "Every man has his price." It means that you can change people's minds by offering them money, or more money. It is what we call a "cynical" remark. It questions the ability of a person to "take a stand" on principle.

Martin Luther, like Martin Luther King after him, like Jesus, (or Paul, or Peter) before him, proves that wrong. Faced by the choice of being obedient to God or running away, they saw it as, really, Hobson's Choice. They had no choice at all.

That is why Jesus died on the cross.

For him, it was "Hobson's Choice".

He couldn't do anything else.

Read 1 Peter 4: 13–19.

I hope you are proud—of your parents, your school, your country, and many other things. It is right to be proud at times.

But there is also a wrong kind of pride. Sometimes we are pleased with ourselves for doing the wrong things!

For example—is there any point in being pleased with ourselves for doing the things it is our duty to do?
Not really!
Jesus made a comment on this. He said of the servants who had carried out their orders, "We are servants and deserve no credit: we have only done our duty" (Luke 17: 10).
Too often we want to have a vote of thanks for doing what we ought to do anyway!
This is not really the right kind of pride.

So the question Jesus really asked was this, "What are you doing MORE than others?" For this is the Christian standard.
We have an obligation as Christians not just to do our duty, but to do more than we are obliged to do.
It is the *more* that a man does that shows he is a Christian.

Read St. Matthew 5: 17–26.

WIDE AS THE WORLD   Day Twenty-two

"We must grow till our arms go round the world."
Who said that?

"Go home and make love grow everywhere."
Who said that?

These sayings come from men who were very different in character, but both had the same vision of the purpose of Christianity.
The first comes from Richard Collier in his great biography of William Booth. He describes the General at a rally of London Salvationists.

"How wide is the girth of the world?" he shouted.

"Twenty-five thousand miles," came the answer.

"Then," roared Booth, "we must grow till our arms get right round about it."

He meant that nothing less than the world for Christ would do.

The second comment comes from a selection from the speeches of Pope John XXIII. It opens with a picture of Pope John on the second night of the Vatican Council, and goes on, "Pope John XXIII stood in the window of his private study, smiling at thousands and thousands of cheering Romans below in St. Peter's Square. He quieted them. He spoke to them. 'Go home,' he said, 'and make love grow from here to everywhere!' "

The accent is the same. Nothing less than a world united in the love of Christ will do.

This universal vision has always been the very centre of the Christian's view of what ought to be.

Read 1 John 3: 11–18.

THE THINGS WE MISS   Day Twenty-three

The things we miss most, when we do not have them, are the simplest things, such as home, friends, work.

There is home.

Nothing can replace home.

To go to school in the morning with no one to say goodbye, to come home in the afternoon with no one there to welcome you is a cold prospect.

A poor home, so long as there is love in it, is happier than the best institution. A poor home or house with love in it is better than all the institutions there are, however sincerely they try to be homes.

We should thank God for institutions and all who run them. But there is no place like home.

There are friends.

There was once a simple Greek man who was on the edge, as it were, of the circle of Socrates and the great ones. One day someone asked him for what he most wished to thank the gods, and he answered, "That being what I am, I have had the friends I have."

Isn't it great to have someone with whom you can argue without quarrelling; someone with whom you do not need to watch what you say; someone to whom you can tell odd things, knowing that he will not laugh at your dreams or criticise your faults or mock at your failures: someone who knows you at your worst and still likes you!

Friendship is a precious thing. And precious are your friends!

There is work.

Hugh Martin once wrote that the saddest words in all Shakespeare are, "Othello's occupation's gone."

John Wesley prayed the famous prayer, "Let me not live to be useless."

It feels as if it would be nice not to have to work!

It isn't.

If you haven't work to do, you will find you are pretty unhappy in life.

God wants you working, not lazing;

> busy, not idle;

> satisfied, not discontented.

It is the man who can work who is the happy man.

Keep working!

Read St. Mark 3: 13–19.

In his book *Then and Now*, John Foster, who was a famous writer and teacher at Glasgow University, tells a story which shows how easy it is to miss a great chance for Jesus.

In 1271, Pope Gregory the Tenth received a request from Kublai Khan, the ruler of the Mongols (which was the widest empire in the East the world has ever seen). Kublai Khan sent Nicolo and Maffeo Polo as his ambassadors to the Pope.

His message ran, "You shall go to your High Priest and shall pray him on our behalf to send me a hundred men skilled in your religion . . . and so I shall be baptised, and, when I shall be baptised, all my barons and great men will be baptised, and then their subjects will receive baptism, and so there will be more Christians here than in your parts."

The whole East was being offered to Jesus! *Yet the Pope did nothing*.

In 1289, Pope Nicholas the Fourth did send missionaries, but they were far too late and far too few.

The chance was lost.

What a difference it would have made if all China and the East had become Christian! History and world politics today would have been very different.

But when God needed them, his men let him down!

Paul said, "We are labourers together with God" (1 Cor. 3: 9).

But are we?

Or are we too likely to lose great opportunities?

Learn from history and look for a chance to serve Jesus.

Read 2 Peter 3: 14–18.

It's great fun giving gifts, because it brings pleasure. But we can give even greater joy if we remember two things.

There is a right time to give a gift. That's the first thing.

When everything is going well and we are feeling prosperous, an extra gift may not make so much difference. But when we are discouraged and disheartened and in trouble, a gift, given in love, may make all the difference in the world.

If you happen to know anyone who is having a bad time at present, it would be a lovely thing to give him or her a small gift—even if it is no more than a word of cheer.

But, secondly, the spirit in which the gift is given is very important.

The cash value of a gift has nothing to do with its value. The value of a gift lies in the love which led the giver to give it. It's the motive that counts.

Many mothers wear a little piece of artificial jewellery with more pride than they would show in relation to a spray of diamonds, just because it was bought with your own money and given with your love.

The most costly gift is valueless, if there is no love in the giving.

The cheapest gift is priceless, if it comes from the love which could give no more.

Once when he was very near the end of his life, a woman gave Jesus a gift. There were those who found fault with the extravagance such love involved.

But Jesus paid her the finest compliment of all when he said, "She has done what she could" (Mark 14: 8).

Read 2 Samuel 24: 18–25.

"MY YOKES FIT WELL!" Day Twenty-six

There is an old legend which tells how Jesus was the best maker of ox-yokes in the whole of Galilee. People came from far and wide to Nazareth to buy the ox-yokes that Jesus of Nazareth made, for they were the best of all, they said.

Jesus was a man who worked with his hands. He was thirty-three when he died on the Cross. For thirty of his thirty-three years he was connected with the carpenter's shop in Nazareth.

One of the most famous and beautiful things that Jesus ever said, goes back to the days when he was a carpenter.
"My yoke is easy," said Jesus, "and my burden is light" (Matt. 11: 30).
The Greek word for easy is *chrestos*, and *chrestos* really means *well-fitting*.

In Palestine ox-yokes were made of wood. The ox would be brought to the carpenter's shop and its measurements would be taken. The yoke would be made, and then the ox would be brought back for a "fit-on".
This curve would be deepened, that rough bit would be smoothed out until the yoke fitted so exactly that it would never gall the backs of the patient beasts.
That was the kind of work Jesus did.
In those days shops had their signs over them just as they have now.
I wonder if the sign above the shop of Jesus was a wooden ox-yoke, with the words painted upon it, "My yokes fit well."

Jesus was not ashamed to work with his hands.
And the work he did with his hands was fine work, I'm sure.

Read St. Mark 1: 1-11.

107

"You need hands . . ."

These are familiar words, I'm sure, because they come from a song often sung by the popular entertainer and comedian, Max Bygraves. And, of course, the song goes on to point out all sorts of ways in which hands are essential.

In fact, your hands work for you all the time. Without them life would, for most of us, be nearly impossible.

You will realise that again when you sit down to your next meal!

Or when you take out toys and games for play.

Or when you want to show your affection to someone.

Yes, indeed, you need hands!

I find working hands specially impressive. To see hands with the marks of hard work on them moves me . . . as it has others.

Thomas Carlyle was one of the most famous of authors. His father was a good, godly man who was an elder in the church. He was a stone-mason.

There are places in Dumfries-shire in southern Scotland where the bridges which Carlyle's father built still stand.

Carlyle said that he would rather have built one of his father's bridges than have written all his own books.

Thomas Carlyle honoured a man who worked with his hands.

Where would a home be without the hands of a mother to cook the meals and scrub the house and care for the children?

How could the dream of the thinker ever be worked out without the hands of the labouring man?

Never, never let us look down on the man who works with his hands. This is awful snobbery. It was the hands of a working-man that were nailed to the Cross on Calvary's hill.

Read Exodus 17: 8–16.

Do you ever wonder *how* you should pray to God?

Well, there are four ways at least in which you can pray to God.

Jesus told of a tax-gatherer who came to the Temple to pray.

He would not even dare to lift up his eyes to heaven, but he hammered on his breast, saying, "God be merciful to me a sinner" (Luke 18: 13).

That is *the prayer of the downcast head*—that is the prayer of the heart that is ashamed. It is the prayer we want to offer when we come to ask God's forgiveness of our wrong-doing.

One of the first ways to pray is to do it in such a way as to say "We are sorry."

Once Abraham Lincoln said, "I have often been driven to my knees in prayer because I had nowhere else to go."

That is *the prayer of the bended knee and the outstretched hand*, the prayer that says, "God help me!"

There are some problems we feel only God can solve.

There are some questions which only God can answer.

There is a strength which only God can give.

There are times when we shall all feel that we have reached the limits in suffering and pain. So we stretch out our hands to God and ask for the strength to cope with our troubles.

I think we shall find God won't let us down!

Read Psalm 124.

DEFENDER OF THE FAITH   **Day Twenty-nine**

In ancient Greece the Spartans were always known for their courage. They might lack the finer virtues of the more cultured Athenians, but no one ever questioned their courage and their loyalty.

In his life of Lycurgus, the Spartan king, Plutarch tells a great story. It goes like this:

There was a certain Spartan wrestler competing at the Olympic Games. An attempt was made to "buy him off" by the offer of a large sum of money. He refused it.

After a long struggle, he outwrestled his opponent and won the victory.

He was asked, "What advantage, O Spartan, have you gained from your victory?"

He answered with a smile, "I shall stand in front of my king when I fight our enemies."

The greatest privilege which the Spartan could imagine was to defend his king, if need be with his life, in the day of battle.

The greatest privilege the Christian has is the privilege of being the "defender of the faith", the champion of Jesus Christ, the one who represents him and defends him in the world.

Will you be that?

Read Romans 1: 8–16.

WHY PRAY?   Day Thirty

Here are two more ways to pray. Think about them.

Once Jesus prayed to God in the garden of Gethsemane, and when he prayed his sweat was as drops of blood.

At that moment the Cross was facing Jesus. He was only thirty-three. No man wants to die as young as that and certainly not on a cross.

Sometimes we know what is right, but it is very hard to do it.

Sometimes we have to face things which are almost too difficult to face.

Sometimes we have to wrestle in prayer until we can say, "Thy will be done."

It is not easy to do.

One of the most gallant exploits of the South African Wars was the defence of Ladysmith.

The leader who was responsible for that brave defence was Sir George White. It was *his* courage, *his* cheerfulness, *his* leadership which made the garrison able to hold out. So when he returned to England, he was a hero.

Everyone was eager to learn the secret of his courage, cheerfulness, and vigour. But he would never say. Then, one day, he was pressed even more strongly than usual to say how he got through the strain and tension of those days of siege. He answered, "Well, if you want to know, every morning every day, I stood at attention before God."

Now, how about that for an answer?

What a difference it would make to life if we always began the day with God; if each day we took our orders from God.

You could not possibly begin a day better than by standing at attention before God, could you?

"More things are wrought by prayer than this world dreams of."

How true—as *you* will find on *your* journey through life.

Read St. Luke 22: 39–46.

MONTH FOUR

I am sure you have heard the phrase, "The Seven Deadly Sins". It is a phrase that comes down from the ancient past.

It describes some of our faults and failings!

At least it is comforting to know that human beings have always had their little failings! So we needn't be too sad when we are not just as good as we would like to be!

The seven worst faults, it seems, were those we know as "The Seven Deadly Sins", and I would like you to think about these this month.

One or two of the thoughts are a little difficult, but it may help you as you grow older to think of these things.

I hope so!

At the head of the list is *pride*!

Pride is, in one sense, the *only* sin, the "parent" sin from which all the other sins come.

Basically, *pride is the exaltation of self.*

I have learned, from being in the doctor's hands, that no one is indispensable! It is so easy for us all to think that the universe revolves round *us*, that *we* are the centre of it all! To give ourselves such importance is dangerous!

Pride is that *self-importance.* If we allow ourselves to begin to think that the world can't go on without us, we can, in the end, make ourselves unable to do the things in which we really are indispensable!

Think of it like this!

You need your mother, but if she takes on all sorts of public duties—including too many church duties—and, if she begins to think that the world cannot get on without her, she may well fail in her duty to her home and to you, her family. Do you see what I mean?

Daddy may get himself so tied up in outside commitments that he does not even know you, his own children.

115

Some of you who have been brought up in manses will know what I mean! "Daddy's at a meeting!" "Daddy's at the Church!"

It is not a bad thing to learn that the world gets on quite well without us, that however important we are, we are not indispensable to everything. That may leave us freer to do the things we really do have to do!

Don't be too self-important!

Read Proverbs 8: 10–13, 16–19.

ENVY   **Day Two**

Let's think today about the sin of *Envy*.
Envy is repeatedly forbidden in the New Testament.

In fact, there are two Greek words there for *envy*, and there is quite a difference in meaning between them.

The first word (and it is the more common one) is the word *phthonos*. The verb it comes from is *phthonein*.

This word is really a word that implies "badness" of some kind. It is a word that just could not be used in a good sense. It really describes an ugly thing.

This was the word that was used by Jewish religious authorities as they brought about the crucifixion of Jesus (Matt. 27: 18; Mark 15: 10).

This word is also used to describe the sin of the false teacher (1 Tim. 6: 4).

It is the sin of what Paul calls a world that does not have Christ in it (Rom. 1: 29; Titus 3: 3). It is something the Christian must "strip off" and "lay aside" for ever (1 Pet. 2: 1).

So you see what an unpleasant feeling that first Greek word (*phthonos*) has.

It is a sinister sort of word.

Read 1 Timothy 6: 1–10.

THE TRAGEDY OF ENVY   Day Three

The second word for *envy* is the word *zelos*. This is the word used when it is said that "love knows no envy" (1 Cor. 13: 4). (It is translated "jealousy" sometimes.)

It is the sin which Paul fears may upset the fellowship of the Corinthian Church (1 Cor. 3: 3; 2 Cor. 12: 20).

It is the sin which must have no part in a Christian's character (James 3: 14, 16).

But in this word (*zelos*) there is one of the real tragedies of life. Envy in the form of *zelos* is not always a bad word. *It can be a noble word*, for it is the word *zeal* in its Greek dress. So it can describe a noble seeking for the highest. It can mean the rise to the heights of our powers—using those words in every sense, physical, mental, and spiritual.

The tragedy is that noble aspiration can so easily turn into ignoble envy, that fine emulation can so easily become evil jealousy! Or, to put it more simply, we want to reach the highest in every way, but our failure to do that may make us envious—in a wrong kind of way—of others, who do better than us. We want to follow the example of someone great, but we are just not able to do it, and so we become jealous of them.

There is such a narrow dividing line between trying to reach the example someone has set up and envying that person because he is better than we are. I'm sure that even at your age you may have felt like this over a schoolmate.

There is no sin as subtle as envy. There is no sin against which we have to be so constantly on guard.

Read James 3: 13–18

BE HONEST!   Day Four

Now that we have seen the background to this word *envy*, we can begin to ask some questions about it.

117

Here is the first point:

How much of our criticism of others is really due to our envy of them?

Sometimes we belittle or jeer at a friend who does well. Why do we do this? Is it because we think we ought to criticise them, or just because we are jealous of them?

One of the things we have to learn in life is to be honest with ourselves in everything. And *envy* is something that should make us do that!

Envy comes from failing to count our own blessings and especially failing to realise that there are things we can do well and do do well! In other words envy can arise in us because we under-value our own talents.

Marshal Foch, a great French general, once said that the whole secret of war is "to do the best one can with the resources one has".

That is also the secret of life. Use the talents you have to the full rather than spend time envying what others are doing with theirs.

There was once a little squirrel who said to the great mountain, "I cannot carry forests on my back, but you cannot crack a nut."

We can all do different things. These things we should do well, and be happy about it.

The root cause of envy is the exaltation of the self.

So long as we think of *our* prestige, *our* importance, *our* reputation, *our* rights, we shall be envious. Envy is very much connected with selfishness and self-centredness.

When we learn to think of our responsibilities and less of our privileges; when we learn to put the emphasis on duties rather than rights, envy will die a natural death.

When we forget ourselves and think of others, then we shall think, not of what *others* have or have not, but of what *we* have and what *others* have not.

The desire to share and to serve is the best way to put an end to envy.

Read St. Mark 10: 35–45.

WRATH

We turn now to the sin that is called *wrath*.

Wrath is, like envy, repeatedly condemned and forbidden in the New Testament.

Twice in Paul's letters two sins are mentioned together and forbidden together, and it is interesting to see the difference between them. If you look up Ephesians 4: 31 and Colossians 3: 8, you will find *wrath* and *anger* are mentioned side by side.

In these two passages wrath is the Greek word *thumos* and anger is *orge*. And in Greek there is a clear distinction between these two words.

Thumos comes from a Greek "root" which means *to boil*, and it describes the anger which blazes up quickly and then just as quickly dies down again.

The Greeks themselves said it was a fire kindled with straw, a fire which crackles and blazes for a very short time and then dies.

So *thumos* is a burst of temper, a blaze of anger, a momentary outbreak of passion.

Orge, on the other hand, is the anger which has become part of us. It describes the anger that lasts for a long time, the frame of mind which "nurses its wrath to keep it warm", the attitude of mind which simply cannot forget or forgive a wrong or an injury. This sometimes means that the anger sometimes goes on all through life. (I can think of people of whom this is true, I'm sorry to say.)

We don't always regard the "quick temper" kind of anger

as very serious. We feel it is so temporary that it can easily be forgotten. The teaching of the New Testament is that the quick blaze of an inflammable temper as well as the long-lasting anger of a bitter heart are *both* to be condemned.

So let us be cautious of our *wrath*—whichever kind it is.

Read Ephesians 4: 26–32.

COUNT TEN! Day Six

Now let us look at wrath a little more closely.

In his letter to the Corinthians, Paul numbers *thumos* (that is the sudden kind of wrath) as one of the things which wrecks a Church (2 Cor. 12: 20).

In his letter to the Galatians, he numbers it among "the sins of the flesh which are opposed to the Spirit" (Gal. 5: 20); it is part of our human nature and not a good part of it!

In his first letter to Timothy, Paul says that, when a man prays, there must be no *orge* (that is the long-lasting anger) in his heart (1 Tim. 2: 8).

James insists that the Christian must be slow to *anger* (*orge*), for the *anger* of man can never work the will of God (James 1: 19, 20).

The Greeks were not really far wrong when they defined anger as "a brief madness". When a man is angry, he is just not in full control of himself. He does things, and says things, to others and *about* others, which, in his calmer moments, he would know to be wrong.

What is more—for it is equally important—even if he does not actually do them or say them, he *thinks* them. Jesus taught that the sin of *thought* is every bit as serious as the sin of action, in his words in the Sermon on the Mount.

Jesus himself said something about anger: "He that is

angry with his brother shall be in danger of the judgment" (Matt. 5: 22).

The Authorised Version of the Bible adds the words "without a cause", but they are in none of the best manuscripts and all the modern versions, from the Revised Version onwards, omit them.

So let's just think about the matter very seriously. There are many people who justify these outbursts of temper and anger by saying that it is their nature, and they cannot help it. If the New Testament is right, they cannot be at one and the same time Christian and bad-tempered or quick-tempered.

Here is some advice, then:

Think before you speak.

Think of the hurt and the harm words cause.

Think of your own sorrow after your anger is over and you regret what you have said.

There is an old Quaker remedy for anger. It is that of counting ten before you speak!

It's good advice.

And of course ask Jesus for help with your anger!

He can give it.

Read James 1: 16–21.

LUST   Day Seven

Now we turn to a difficult word. It is *lust*. But it is important that we should understand why lust is wrong and what it does to people.

First we must try to be clear about the meaning of the word *lust*.

Lust tends to be associated almost entirely with wrong desires of a physical kind, especially connected with sex, but it has a far wider meaning than that.

Lust is the desire for *anything*. It is our wanting something we have a right to have and want, but doing it in a wrong way.

Lust is a right desire wrongly used.

Now I know that will be difficult for you to understand, but let's try to look at it more closely.

There is a physical lust, that is when people want to possess someone else's body. But they want it for *selfish* reasons.

The fault in physical lust and in immorality is that they *deliberately use other people as a means of satisfying entirely selfish desires*.

Any relationship between two people, whatever age they are, if it is to be a *Christian* relationship, must be a *partnership*. Any relationship in which one person does all the taking and another all the giving is wrong. And *that* is what lust seeks to do.

Strangely enough, Christians have often spoken as if they regarded the body as evil in some way, and that therefore anything to do with sex was evil. (This is, of course, not what God intended. Our bodies are good!) Yet the practice of having unmarried priests has developed in some branches of the Church. Monasteries came to be a feature of Christian life because of the fear of the body.

But Jesus did not condemn marriage, or love, or sex— quite the opposite. He believed there was no higher form of relationship than that of love and marriage (Matt. 19: 3–9).

I think, too, that the fact that St. Paul spoke of the relationship between God and his church as if it was like a marriage shows that he too felt how valuable marriage was.

Don't look on your body as if it was "bad" or "evil".

It is the body God gave you.

It is as St. Paul said in a rather lovely phrase, the "temple" in which God's spirit can dwell.

Read 1 Cor. 3: 11–17.

When does love become lust? This is the next question in our thinking together on the difficult subject of *lust*.

Love becomes *lust* when one person wishes to use another person simply to satisfy his own desire. If two people love each other, that love has to be a partnership of *body*, *mind* and *spirit*. It must be a real and total *partnership*, in which each partner finds a new completeness in life with the other.

When one person does no more than use another person to satisfy physical instincts, then love becomes lust.

Do you understand this? It is so important today when sadly so much that is called love is really only lust.

Now here is something important, too. There is a "spiritual lust". This is a very difficult phrase for you to understand. But let's try.

Spiritual lust can be seen in what we often call ambition, the desire "to get to the top", the desire for power over other people, the desire to *use* other people for our own personal private ends and purposes. We sometimes talk of all this as "the rat race". In this we simply mean that life seems to consist of people "getting on" by trampling on other people.

Here again the fault is exactly the same! Our relationship with other people *must* be that of partnership. Whenever we make use of them, or try to use them as means towards an end; whenever our aim is to get things *out of* them rather than to share things *with them*, then spiritual lust has entered in.

It is right that you should make the best of your gifts. You must want to make the biggest contribution to life that you possibly can. But the basis of your desire must not be *selfish*. It must be selfless. It should not be the desire to get, but the desire to give. It should not be *isolation from* men but *identity with* men.

The Christian word is a Greek word, *koinonia*, and *koinonia* means *fellowship*. It means partnership. It means an attitude of mind in which you always think of yourself as bound up with others.

So long as you keep before you this idea of partnership, of fellowship, of sharing, of "identifying" yourself with others, you will be in no danger of either physical or spiritual lust.

I know this has been a difficult thought, but I hope I have helped you to see the real tragedy which *lust* is.

You need never be ashamed to *love*: you should always be ashamed of *lust*.

Read 1 Corinthians 13: 1–8a.

GLUTTONY

Day Nine

The next "deadly sin" is *gluttony*.

This is, perhaps, one we ought to think about because we do all like food!

Let's look at gluttony in relation to Aristotle's "golden mean".

Aristotle described every virtue as "the mean" between two extremes. On the one hand he said there was the extreme of "excess", and on the other the extreme of "defect". In between, there is the "golden mean", or as we would rather call it, the "happy medium".

Let's take an example. *Recklessness* would be one extreme—the extreme of excess. *Cowardice* would be the extreme of defect. The golden mean between this would be *courage*.

There are three ways of looking at ways of satisfying our bodies. The first is summed up in a big and difficult word—asceticism.

Asceticism is the way of looking at things which believes that the body should be deliberately starved and ill-treated.

124

To eat at all is felt to be a bad thing! The perfect ideal would be to eliminate food from life altogether!

This was the attitude of the monks and the hermits of the early Church, when they left the company of men and went out to live in the desert. I doubt if it is an attitude that appeals to any of us!

H. B. Workman, in a book called *The Evolution of the Monastic Ideal*, quotes some examples of the way in which the monks and hermits in the Egyptian deserts lived.

> Some passed days without food—the trial fast of Paul the Simple, when applying to Anthony that he might join the hermits, lasted four days—while others never partook of food until sunset. In the week before Easter some kept an almost unbroken fast ... Some never drank except upon rare occasions. Adolius, a Syrian monk of Jerusalem, only broke his fast during Lent one day in five. A Cilician hermit named Conon for thirty years only had one meal a week.

It is said that a certain Ptolemaeus lived for five years on the dew that he collected with a sponge from stones!

And the famous Simon Stylites spent all *his* time on a little platform at the top of a pillar.

That is very extreme, the extreme defect, and there is no justification for it in the New Testament.

Jesus was happy to be at a wedding reception and, when the multitude were hungry, his first thought was to give them food, and food in plenty.

So asceticism is not the answer God wants us to adopt as to how we should think of our bodies.

Read St. John 6: 1–14.

We saw that asceticism is the "extreme of defect" in relation to our attitude to our bodies. *Gluttony* is the extreme of excess!

Gluttony is over-indulgence in food.

In New Testament times, a wave of refined gluttony swept over the Roman Empire. It was the time when men sat down to feasts of peacocks' brains and nightingales' tongues; when a certain Roman Emperor succeeded in spending a million and a half pounds on food in eighteen months; when good food became a sort of god and eating became the most important thing in life.

Gluttony is eating for eating's sake. It is living to eat instead of eating to live.

The "extreme of excess" is just such a *gluttony*.

Then thirdly, there is *enjoyment*, and this is really the "golden mean".

One of the great sayings in the Bible speaks of God "who giveth us richly all things to enjoy" (1 Tim. 6: 17).

If we accept this *principle of enjoyment*, everything begins to fall into place. We shall know how to use *all food and drink*.

Enjoyment involves a wise, temperate, disciplined use of all good gifts.

It will mean that there are good reasons for abstaining occasionally even from good things. In other words, the idea of *fasting* can be a useful practice.

There is sense in the use of a certain amount of fasting. If we are able to lay aside a pleasure for a time, it means that we have not become dependent on it. And we shall enjoy a return to it.

We ought to be in control of our appetites and not let our appetites be in control of us.

So let us sum all this up by saying that the Christian way

avoids both asceticism and gluttony, but remembers that God gave us all things richly to enjoy.

Eat to live, but don't live to eat.

It is *gluttony* if you do just that.

Read 1 Timothy 6: 10–19.

AVARICE Day Eleven

Some sins are very attractive, and some aren't. And *avarice* is the least attractive of all the sins!

None of you would wish to be known as greedy. None of you would want to grow up to be a miser.

Avarice need not end in your being that, however. *Avarice* is simply an illegitimate greed for money.

Now *avarice* grows from some wrong ideas about money and about what money can do. I'd like to look at these with you, because they are important.

First, it grows from a wrong idea of the meaning of the word "enough".

"Enough" has been defined as always being "a little more than a man has"! Do you get the point? In other words, we always want just that little bit more than we have.

The curious thing about money is that, however much we have, we feel everything in the garden would be lovely if only we had a little more. So people try to get the little more, and then want just a little more! And more! And more!

Epicurus, who was a philosopher in ancient Greece, said something which shows a real knowledge of what we are all like. "If you wish to make a man happy, add not to his possessions, but take away from his desires . . . To whom little is not enough," he said, "*nothing is enough.*"

Money is valuable. You will need it in life and you have a right to want it. Poverty is not a blessing. Even sorrow (as the proverb puts it) is easier to bear when there is a loaf of bread to hand.

But do let us remember that for those who think only in terms of money, "enough" can never be reached.

We shall always want more!

That is really what *avarice* is all about.

Read St. Luke 19: 11–26.

TRUE CONTENT   Day Twelve

Looking a bit more at avarice, this is the next thing we must say.

Avarice grows from a wrong idea of what happiness is all about.

However much possessions and money help us towards happiness, when we already have some of it, they do not themselves create happiness.

The Greeks had their own version of the story of Midas and Phrygia.

Midas loved money, so he asked the gods to give him the ability to turn everything he touched into gold. They granted his request.

It was wonderful! He touched the flowers and they became gold. He touched the cups and plates and they became gold. And so did everything else.

Then he was hungry and looked forward to his supper, but no sooner did he touch the food and the drink set before him, than it became solid gold too!

His little daughter ran into the room. Before he could stop her, she ran and kissed him. She became a little statue of solid gold.

Midas pleaded with the gods to take the gift away!

Do you know the poem about the king who was dying of melancholy?

He was told that the only thing that could possibly save him was for him to get the shirt of a perfectly happy man and wear it.

His servants searched from one end to another of the kingdom for such a man.

He was found at last. He was a tramp on the roads. He had no shirt to his back!

Often money in plenty brings not happiness, but worry.
Money is not the way in which you can buy happiness.
Happiness is something you have, not something you buy.
I hope *you* find it.
And value it.

Read St. Luke 16: 19–31.

TRUE SECURITY   Day Thirteen

Now a final thought about *avarice*.

Avarice springs from the idea that money is the source of our security. Many people feel that to have plenty of money is to be able to enjoy life and to feel safe.

I'm not sure that is really true.

Jesus, you remember, told the story of the man whose barns were simply bursting. He sat back saying to himself, "Eat, drink and be merry." But, to use the Bible words, his "soul was suddenly required of him." In other words, he died. He couldn't take his wonderful possessions then. They weren't of any use to him at that time.

So Jesus said rightly, though gently, "A man's life does not consist in the abundance of his possessions" (Luke 12: 13–21).

The strange thing about the sin of *avarice* and the desire

for too much money is that when we really think about it, and when we see what it all really means, we wonder how on earth anyone could be so stupid as to be guilty of greed.

We all, older and younger, need to remember that it is folly to lay up treasure on earth. We do not live "by bread alone", as Jesus told Satan in his time of temptation.

Money isn't everything.
It's not even the most important thing in life.
There's far more to life than that.
I do hope *you* find it!

Read Proverbs 11: 1–6.

SLOTH Day Fourteen

In modern lists of the seven deadly sins, the seventh sin is called *sloth*. If we look at older lists, however, we will find it is called by another rather curious name: *accidie*.

Accidie was once a common English word. It was used, for instance, in the time of the great English poet, Chaucer. It has dropped out of our modern language. And there is really no one word in modern English that will express exactly what it means.

The sin which *accidie* describes may not have a definite name, but nowadays it is still easily recognised, because many people have experienced it.

One of the best descriptions of it is by a man called John Cassian. He describes *accidie* as it affects people like monks and hermits.

Accidie, he says, describes a frame of mind in which you begin to dislike the place where you are and despise the people with whom you work or live.

You feel everything would be so much better if only you

could get into a better place and move amongst more Christian people.

You feel that you are not getting anywhere, so you begin to think you are really of no use to anyone and that you would never be missed.

So, in the end, you become idle and unable to concentrate on anything. You wander about looking for someone to talk to, not able to work yourself and unwilling to let anyone else work. You grow "wraure" (that is an old English word used by Chaucer which means peevish and unpleasant).

Now this may not be something which boys and girls feel, but it is useful to know of the sin and how it can grow.

Accidie is boredom. It's as simple as that.

It is the attitude of the person who is "fed-up" with life, people and everything.

It is the attitude of those who can't be bothered with anything, the people who, as we say, just "couldn't care less".

So *accidie* is an unpleasant sort of attitude.

I hope *you* will never experience it.

Read Proverbs 6: 6–11.

YOU CAN'T BE BORED   Day Fifteen

Accidie, or *sloth*, is much much worse than just plain laziness, as I think you will agree, after all we said yesterday.

There is a streak of laziness in all of us, I'm afraid. *Accidie* is the attitude of the person who has simply lost the joy of living, working and meeting people. He (or she) has even lost the joy of worship and prayer. He is bored with life in general and there is nothing worth doing and nothing left to live for.

131

Actually, it is a very common attitude today. I often see it in young people who, at a very early age, are utterly bored with life.

I remember hearing a certain doctor say that boredom is *the* modern illness, and that he believed that medicine would find a cure for cancer long before it would find the answer to boredom.

The Christian should never be bored. There is far too much in life for that to be possible.

I think the person who has fallen into this sin of *accidie* has forgotten two things.

First he has forgotten why he ever came into this world.

Everyone in this world has a job to do for God. God wants him—or her—to do something specific for him. There is a reason for us being here, and we have got to find it.

What God wants us to do need not be a task which is great as the world calls things great. It may be simply to make someone else happy, to cure someone's body, to bring sunshine into the lives of those on the other side of the counter or in the office, to make a home.

As Robert Burns, the great Scottish poet put it:

> To make a happy friendship clime
>   For weans and wife—
> That's the true pathos and sublime
>   Of human life.

It may seem strange that the seven deadly sins end with the sin of boredom. Perhaps you have never felt that being bored is a sin at all. But when a man remembers his work for God in the world, boredom can never really enter his life.

The Christian life is exciting.

As God meant it to be.

Read 2 Thessalonians 3: 6–13.

Have you heard of the very big word "sanctification"? It was used a lot in our churches when I was young but "sanctification" seems to have dropped out of our vocabulary now!

The Greek word for sanctification is *hagiasmos*. All Greek nouns which end in *-asmos* describe a process that is going on, so *hagiasmos* could in fact be translated, in a rather lovely phrase, *the road to holiness*.

Each day in our lives we ought to be a little further along the road to holiness, the road to loveliness, the road to beauty. But sometimes we are stuck in one place and find we are no better than we were a day, a week, a month, a year ago.

If we are going to make any progress at all along the way to holiness and beauty, there are some things we really need.

First we need a bit of self-examination, that is, we need to look at what we are and what we are doing.

A writer has said that there is something wrong with life, if we have "no time to stand and stare". That is true, but we should not only take time to stand and stare *at the world.* Every now and again we should take a good look *at ourselves*.

The famous Dr. Johnson, whom we have quoted before, used to say, that Sunday ought to be used for self-examination, and that we should always examine ourselves to see if we are a little farther on than we were last week.

Of course, we don't want to do this sort of thing as if we were hopeless creatures. We are not! But sometimes it is necessary just to see what we are like, what we are doing— and what effect we are having on others.

> "O wad some po'er* the giftie gie us
> To see oorsels as ithers see us!"

said Robert Burns in his Scottish accent.

* "power".

It will do us good to look at ourselves and be aware of our faults.

Then we can perhaps make ourselves a little better, and move a pace forward on the road to holiness.

Read Galatians 5: 16–25.

DEPENDENT, YET INDEPENDENT   Day Seventeen

One of the hero stories of modern times is the story of the Scottish poet, William Soutar. He died in 1943 at the very early age of forty-five.

He died after twenty-five years of illness and ten years of complete helplessness.

In fact he was so ill that there was a time when he could do nothing more than move his head.

That situation Soutar met with gallantry.

When at twenty-five he knew that he could not live very long, he said, "Now I can be a poet."

When he became as helpless as a little child, he said, "One's core of manliness must be preserved."

"Life," he said, "demands something more from a man than a handful of lyrics."

Life received more from the brave William Soutar.

The story of that life has been beautifully written by Alexander Scott in his biography entitled *Still Life*.

Here are two sayings of Soutar's quoted in that book:

The first is an incident related by Soutar himself. He was thinking of his earliest memories and he describes the "first important symbolic episode in his life," just because it had meant so much to him.

He and his mother had set out for a walk one afternoon when he was about three years old. Suddenly the walk was interrupted, when the little lad ran from his mother with the words which he flung over his shoulder, "Get back, get back, I don't require a mother."

That was the rebel longing for independence as so many of you do. But this very same William Soutar was in his life to say later, "If I have been privileged to catch a more comprehensive glimpse of life than many other men, it is because I have stood on the shoulders of my parents."

That is the declaration, not of independence, but of dependence!

So we need both, don't we? We need to stand on our own feet. But we also need to stand on our parents' shoulders!

Read 1 Samuel 2: 12–20.

SALT THE PORRIDGE! Day Eighteen

William Soutar was not only a great poet. He was also a writer of quite beautiful prose and very often it had wit and humour in it.

Sometimes he used to write parables.
Here is one of them.

There was once a wood-cutter's wife who forgot to salt her husband's porridge, and when the woodman reproved her she retorted that he was a fool to make a fuss about so small a thing. This angered the woodman and, coming to his task, he began to smite at a tree furiously, so that in a backswing his axe-head flew off to a great distance and injured a favourite horse of his master's which was being led to be reshod. Now on that day this very horse was to have borne the nobleman to a meeting of noblemen who were gathering to discuss their grievances against the king. It was therefore in a disgruntled mood that the woodcutter's master joined his peers; and under compulsion of his anger,

135

eloquently counselled his confederates to revolt. In the subsequent tumult many were slain by the sword, pestilence and famine; and for a generation afterwards the people bowed under the burden of great taxation.

All because a woodman's wife forgot to salt the porridge, there was rebellion and a long time of suffering!

That parable is a parable of the greatness of little things. "Who hath despised the day of small things?" said Zechariah (Zech. 4: 10).

Yes, small things matter. "Behold how great a matter a little fire kindleth," James says. Or perhaps you may like this sentence in a variation noted in the New English Bible. It reads, "What a huge fire starts from a small spark" (James 3: 5–6).

So don't despise the little gift or talent you have to offer. It could lead to a great deal of good as your life develops.

Read Zechariah 4: 8–10.

BE SERENE!   **Day Nineteen**

Let's think a little more about the importance of little things.
There are times when small things can save a man.
This was something William Soutar found out himself. In his increasing helplessness, it was inevitable that more and more things became impossible for him.
He writes, "So much can wither away from the human spirit, and yet the great gift of the ordinary day remains; the stability of the small things of life, which yet in their constancy are the greatest."
Again and again you will find joy and happiness in the everyday things. In sorrow, worry, indecision, there is

136

nothing which helps people so much as having to go on with the ordinary routine of life.

The worst possible thing is to sit down amid regrets and do nothing but worry. That's fatal!

Ordinary duties make us go on.

And that's good!

There are times when small things can ruin life.

A habit that develops from the smallest of things can spoil life.

The point of William Soutar's parable is the way in which small things can cause widespread disaster.

Lose a collar stud and a man can go out in a frame of mind which means trouble for a whole office, or class, or shop!

A tiny upset can make a woman start a day in a way which makes the whole family unhappy.

A dispute, an argument, a difference at a breakfast-table can produce repercussions all over a city in the various places in which members of the family work.

If we are to make life happy for ourselves and for others, we must learn something of the great virtue of serenity.

We can learn that from Jesus more than in any other way.

Read 1 Corinthians 14: 6–10.

LIVE EXCITINGLY! Day Twenty

There are many creatures in this world whose life-span is far beyond our human life-span. Man is by no means the living creature with the longest life on earth!

So length of life is not really the most important thing about life, is it?

Just think of this again!

Poets like Shelley, Keats, Rupert Brooke; musicians like

Schubert and Mozart all died long before they had reached even middle age.

Jesus died at thirty-three.

Here is an important thing to say about life.
The value of a life lies in the intensity of its living.
Do you understand what that means? It means that it is better to live for a shorter time with passionate intensity, stretching out eager hands to grasp all that is good in life, enjoying life to the uttermost, living life to the full, than it is to live for a much longer time with care and prudence and always being careful not to be excited or to do too much.

Sir Walter Scott wrote these lines as a chapter heading in his famous book *Old Mortality*:

> Sound, sound the clarion, fill the fife;
>   To all the sensual world proclaim,
> One crowded hour of glorious life
>   Is worth an age without a name.

You will do people an awful lot of good in *your* lifetime if you make it a joy for them to be alive.

To do this, you yourselves must get a real thrill out of living.

So live excitingly and help others to live too!

Read Acts 7: 54–60.

LOSE IT!   **Day Twenty-one**

Here is something else we must say about life.
The value of a life lies in the way in which it is spent, not in the way in which it is hoarded.
This is really like Jesus saying that to save your life, you must lose it!

The people whom the world remembers with real thankfulness are the people who gave of themselves freely rather than the careful souls who jealously guarded their lives lest they should strain themselves!

Philip James Bailey's epic, *Festus*, is long since forgotten except for its four famous lines:

We live in deeds, not years, in thoughts, not breaths;
In feelings, not in figures on a dial.
We should count time by heart-throbs. He most lives
Who thinks most, feels the noblest, acts the best.

The real question in life is not how we have managed to save life, but how we have managed to spend it! Yes, Jesus was right. If you set out to save life, you lose it, but if you lose it, you find it!

Life is the one possession in which extravagance in your attitude to living is better than economy.

And a final saying:
In assessing the value of any life, it must always be added to the reckoning that no life stops here.

Rita Snowden, a very famous writer of children's stories and books, tells of two workmen who were discussing the death of Dick Sheppard, a famous London vicar, who was also the friend of the people, and who died—from the human point of view—too soon.

"Poor Dick Sheppard's dead," said the first.

"None of your *poor* Dick Sheppard," said the other. "God will be real glad to have him."

So let's say it again with Jesus:

"Whoever shall seek to save his life shall lose it; and whoever shall lose his life shall preserve it" (Luke 17: 33).

It's so true!

Read 2 Timothy 4: 9–22.

Do you find really hard work impossible? Well, I have to
say it! You won't get anywhere in life without real effort.

Sometimes we think great people—writers, thinkers,
leaders—didn't have to try hard. But they did!

Just look at these facts!

Horace, the great Roman writer, advised all authors to
keep what they had written beside them for nine years
before they published it. Nine years! It's a long, long time!
And certainly nowadays, change in life is so constant,
everything would be out of date! But you see what he
means!

Plato's Republic begins with a simple sentence. "I went
down to the Piraeus yesterday with Glaucon, the son of
Ariston, that I might offer up prayer to the goddess." Yet
on Plato's own manuscript and in his own hand-writing,
there are *thirteen different versions of that single sentence*. He
worked at that sentence until every word and phrase was
absolutely right!

Thomas Gray's "Elegy" is one of the poems you probably
learn at school. It was *begun* in the summer of *1742*, but it
was not until June 12, *1750* that it was shown even within
the circle of Gray's friends. It took eight years to achieve
these few immortal verses.

"Sweat, tears, toil." This was what Sir Winston Churchill
offered to the people of Great Britain in 1940. Victory (he
said) couldn't come without every possible effort by
everyone.

Life, fortunately, doesn't always have to be like that. But
it is still true that real success in life—or for that matter,
the Christian life—calls for real effort.

Keep trying!

Read 1 Thessalonians 5: 8–13.

We talked yesterday about the need to struggle and strive in order to learn. To do this needs discipline, and in fact self-discipline. We have to make ourselves do things.

The most tragic example of indiscipline in English literature is the career of Samuel Taylor Coleridge. He had such a great mind, but he did little with it.

Coleridge left Cambridge to join the army. He left the army because, with all his learning, he could not rub down a horse! He went to Oxford and left without getting a degree.

He began a paper called the *Watchman* which ran for ten issues and then just couldn't go on.

It has been said of Coleridge, "He had every gift save one —the gift of sustained and concentrated effort."

He said himself that he had all sorts of books ready for printing "except for transcription". He just would not face the discipline of writing them down.

Don't you find it rather sad that a man who could have been so great was so lacking in self-discipline? This is real tragedy. It's what the word tragedy truly means.

Discipline yourself to work hard.

If you don't do that, the streets in your life may be paved with good intentions! But in the end all you will have are the intentions and nothing real to show for them!

It's worth struggling to succeed.

It's worth the self-discipline it needs to achieve success and, even more, satisfaction.

Read 2 Timothy 2: 15–21.

While Dr. Lewis Cameron was a lecturer in Agriculture in Leeds, he spent a holiday in Aberdeen. Some friends invited him, and the lady who was to be his wife, to come to the evening service in Holburn United Free Church, at which a famous preacher, Dr. A. W. Scuddamore Forbes of the West Parish Church of St. Nicholas was to preach.

In a church which could seat a thousand people, there were about forty people present.

Dr. Forbes preached on the text, "Jonah rose up to flee unto Tarshish from the presence of the Lord" (Jonah 1: 3).

Suddenly Dr. Forbes laid aside his sermon notes and said, "Why are all these pews empty? The people, like Jonah, fled from the presence of the Lord, refusing to face his challenge. Why are our Divinity Halls empty? Young men are more concerned about their own material advantages and selfish pleasures than with the advancement of the Kingdom of God!"

In that moment something happened to Lewis Cameron. He decided to enter the ministry.

So however important or unimportant it was that there should be forty people scattered around one church, what matters is that one man's life was changed!

Dr. Cameron—his story is told in *Opportunity My Ally* (Saint Andrew Press)—became a great figure in the life of the Church of Scotland.

Read St. Matthew 18: 19–20.

OR BY FEW   Day Twenty-five

One Sunday evening in January 1946 Lewis Cameron set off from Edinburgh for St. Luke's Church, Milngavie. It was snowing hard. It was doubtful if he would get through and he only did it by following a snow plough.

When he got to the church, he found that the heating system had broken down and there was only a handful of people in a very cold building. He spoke on the work his church did to help people in need, but it seemed hardly worth while.

The next morning he received a 'phone call from a Glasgow lawyer who helped to look after a certain "trust" or fund. As a result of that sermon to a handful of people in a freezing church on a snowy January night, the Church of Scotland received £104,226 for its social work.

Only a few people heard—but what a result!

Numbers are not all-important. It can be in the smallest congregation that the biggest things happen.

Jesus told us that, where "two or three are gathered together", he will be there in spirit, too. And his presence can create miracles.

God's miracles are not dictated by numbers.

Few or many, God is there.

And if God is there, miracles can happen!

And do!

As Lewis Cameron discovered.

Read St. Matthew 18: 1–6.

GIVE THEM A HAND! Day Twenty-six

I go to football matches when I can. I happened to be in London once when two of the most famous clubs in England were playing, so I went to see the match.

It was a thriller.

One of the clubs was a very famous club which had been doing very badly. In order to get back on the rails, they had signed on some new young players for very large transfer fees.

It is very difficult for a young player, in that situation, to show he is really worth his colossal transfer fee. He is always conscious of what the club paid for him.

One of these young footballers was playing as a striker, and he was trying as hard as he could to do well. He did get one magnificent goal, but a little later he missed an easy chance. He shot the ball past an open goal from about three yards.

He stood there absolutely dejected, his head down.

In the same forward line there was a midfield player who was a famous international. He had played for that particular club for a long time. When this famous international saw the sadness of his young colleague, he ran up to him, put a comforting arm round his shoulder, gave him a pat on the back, and said some words of encouragement to him. The young striker squared his shoulders, shook himself, and played the game twice as hard as he had done before.

Isn't this an example to all of us?

"Brethren," said Paul, "if a man be overtaken in a fault, you who are spiritual, restore such an one in the spirit of meekness; considering yourself, lest you also be tempted" (Gal. 6: 1).

If somebody is feeling down or sad, comfort him or her. Give them a hand.

This is surely the Christian way.

Read Galatians 6: 1–5.

UNDERSTAND! Day Twenty-seven

One of the most famous politicians of all time was William Gladstone.

Once, in the House of Commons, Gladstone made a most important speech. In it he had to quote certain figures, and the figures he quoted were quite inaccurate.

His opponents seized on his mistake and made things very difficult for him.

The figures had been supplied to Gladstone by his private

secretary. It was the duty of the secretary to brief his chief, so Gladstone might well have been very angry with that young man for involving him in such a public mistake. He might even have wanted to get rid of him.

Instead, that night Gladstone wrote him a very kind and understanding letter telling him not to worry. He knew that everybody made mistakes, that, as far as he was concerned, the matter would never be mentioned again.

That was a wonderful action by a very great man. I'm sure that secretary never forgot what Mr. Gladstone had done.

We should all try to be understanding and forgiving when people do make mistakes. If great men like Mr. Gladstone could, so can we.

And, of course, to be understanding and forgiving like this is to be like God.

For we make mistakes.

And he understands.

As we forgive, may we be forgiven!

Read St. Luke 7: 40–43.

"BELIEVISM"   Day Twenty-eight

John Newton had done a lot of wrong things.

In his youth he had reached a very low level, on land and as a sailor on the ship of a slave-trader. But every now and again something would happen, a thunder-storm or a hurricane, and John Newton would turn to God and ask his help.

Then he would forget and his bad life would engulf him. Again and again John Newton writes, "I forget; I so soon forgot."

We are all a bit like that, aren't we? The moment we are sorry, we forget.

We forget *so* soon.

We can all reach heights of goodness, but we can all just as easily let God—and ourselves—down.

Heine was a German writer. He had not been a good man, and yet he never seemed in the least worried about it. When he was asked why he was so unworried, he answered, "God will forgive. *C'est son métier." It is his trade.*

Because God is so forgiving, we are apt to take advantage of him.

But the New Testament is clear. "Bring forth therefore fruits meet for repentance" (Matt. 3: 8). "By their fruits ye shall know them" (Matt. 7: 20). We are to be sorry for our sins. And we must show our sorrow to be sincere.

Someone has complained about what he called the danger of "only believism". He meant that it's not enough to say we believe in God, we have to show our belief in our actions.

He is right!

Read St. Matthew 3: 5–12.

FIRE!   Day Twenty-nine

We once had a fire in our house. It was bad enough to bring out the fire-brigade.

The paraffin stove in my study went up in flames. The fault was mine, not the stove's!

My wife and I were able to put the flames out so that the worst of the danger was averted. But the stove itself, and the rugs in which we had smothered it, were still smouldering, so for safety's sake we decided to telephone for the fire-brigade.

I rang 999 and told the voice at the other end my trouble.

146

The answer came back immediately, "We'll deal with it."
In six minutes the fire-brigade arrived.

The firemen did deal with the situation efficiently and also courteously (they even asked for something with which to wipe up the mess!), and the situation which might have caused a very great deal of damage was cleared up with hardly any damage at all.

This experience taught me a lot.

I discovered, for example, that, in certain circumstances in life, if you are wise, *you shout for help*. You may feel very silly about it but, if you want to avoid worse trouble, you do ask for help!

It should be like that with God. Many problems in life come from the fact that we try to do things by ourselves, when we ought to call in the help of God. Call! He will hear!

I also learned this.

For many years I have seen on my telephone the words, "Emergency Calls. For fire, police or ambulance dial 999." I have never had to dial 999 before, and I often wondered what would happen if I did! Now I know! It works! There is help at the end of the line! The link is sound.

We can make the same discovery about God. We know God is there. We have been told that, if we call upon him, he helps. But perhaps we have never tried it out. If we call on God, and ask for his help, we shall find that, like dialling 999, it works, too.

He is there.

At the end of our prayer link.

Read Psalm 126.

A SOUND LINK Day Thirty

I discovered more as a result of that fire!
I discovered that, when I asked for help, *it came with*

147

speed. This is true in the experience of many people, too. When we ask for God's help, time and time again God answers, and answers at once.

One of the loveliest things in life is the way that a mother hears a child's cry in the night. Mother may be asleep, but just let the child utter a sound, and immediately Mother wakes up and runs to see what is wrong.

"Before they call," says God, "I will answer; and while they are yet speaking, I will hear" (Isaiah 65: 24).

I discovered yet another thing!

Once all the bother was finished, and there was time to speak to the firemen, I felt very apologetic about it all. I was specially apologetic that I had sent for the fire-brigade when the worst was over, and there was nothing left but the smouldering remains to deal with.

But the firemen insisted that I had done the right thing.

"If you are in the slightest doubt," they said, "never hesitate to send for us. *That is what we are here for.*"

When in doubt, call for help.

Whether it's for the fire-brigade.

Or for God's help.

He never "slumbers or sleeps" (it says in Psalm 121). He is always there.

He wants us to know he will never let us down.

Read Isaiah 40: 1–11.

THE BOOK   Day Thirty-one

We had a routine visit from the officer of the salvage corps after we had the fire in our house. He came into my study; he made a note of the trifling damage, and looked at my desk. My Bible was lying there open.

"I see you've got the Book," he said. "You'll not come to much harm so long as you have got it there."

Now I don't know that man's name, but out of our fire there came again a great truth, which I value and I hope you will value, too.

There are things which can wreck a life even more disastrously than a fire can wreck a house. But they will not get the chance to wreck life, so long as we have *the Book*. For having "the Book" means we have knowledge of the God of which "the Book" tells.

With that knowledge, we don't need to be afraid.

Read Revelation 1: 1–3; and St. John 20: 24–25.

MONTH FIVE

I expect you have heard of the Scottish "clans". They were the old and important family divisions of Scotland, and people were (and are!) very proud of their clan associations!

They usually also had a particular colour of tartan (or mixture of colour patterns) and they had a clan motto.

It's the mottoes I would like to think about with you for a part of this month.

First the *Macmillans*.

The Macmillans come from several parts of Scotland. They come from Knapdale in Argyllshire and from Galloway in the south-west as well.

Perhaps they began by being a family of holy men connected with the Church, for it may be that the name of Macmillan is connected with the Gaelic word *moal*, which means *bald* or *tonsured*. And monks are often tonsured—that is, shaven on the head.

The Macmillans have a marvellous Latin motto—*Miserie succurrere disco*. It means, "I learn to succour the wretched", or, as we might put it, "I learn to help the unhappy".

There could be few finer mottoes than that, could there?

If we are to learn to "help the unhappy", then we must remember certain things. For example:

We must learn to see the unhappiness of others.

It is easy to go through life not even noticing the pain and the sorrow that people have.

In the old days in America, Dwight L. Morrow was a very influential man who played a great part in making the decisions as to whom his party would "run" as President. He had a daughter called Anne Morrow. When she was a child she used to be present at some very important gatherings—though she was seldom noticed.

At one meeting the question arose as to whether or not a man called Calvin Coolidge was a good candidate for the Presidency.

Coolidge had been interviewed, and had left the meeting, so now they were discussing whether or not he would do!

Anne's voice interrupted the discussions of the statesmen.

"Of course he'll do," she said.

Her father asked her why she was so sure.

She lifted up a rather grubby thumb decorated by an even more grubby bandage.

"He is the only one of you," she said, "who noticed that I had a sore thumb, and who asked me how it was getting on."

How right she was!

"To help the unhappy" is a good aim and motto.

Read St. Luke 7: 11–17.

SEE, FEEL, ACT!   Day Two

How can we "help the unhappy"?

Here is the answer. *We must learn to* feel *the unhappiness of others.*

You see, it is not enough just *to see*. When we *see*, we must also *feel*. It is possible to *see* the unhappiness of others and to think it has nothing to do with us. It's not *our* concern.

A man called William Morris used to say that, every time he passed a drunk man in the street, he really felt it was in some way his fault that he was in that state.

It is what we call a "hard heart" that doesn't feel others' suffering. But there is something else we must do.

We must learn to act to help others. To see is not enough; even to feel is not enough; the *seeing* and the *feeling* must be turned into *action*. There is a very special reason for that.

St. Francis of Assisi as a young man loved pleasure. One day he was out riding when he saw a leper, in rags, alone and badly disfigured.

Up to that time Francis had thought of nothing but pleasure, but something made him lean down from his horse and throw his arms around that human being in sympathy and love. As he did so, the figure in his arms seemed to change into Jesus himself.

"Inasmuch as you have done it unto one of the least of these my brethren," said Jesus, "you have done it unto me" (Matt. 25: 40). How often we think of these words, yet how true they are!

The help any of us give to a "brother" in trouble is help given to Jesus Christ. That is why every Christian should have as his motto: "I learn to help the unhappy, I learn to succour the wretched."

Read St. Matthew 25: 31–45.

UNCONQUERED   Day Three

Liddlesdale, in the Border Country, is the ancestral home of the *Armstrongs*.

At one time they were so strong that King James the Fifth decided to put down their lawlessness personally, as it were.

He arranged a meeting with John Armstrong of Gilnockie. When Armstrong arrived with his retinue, King James exclaimed, "What wants you, knave, that a king should have?"

The motto of the Armstrong's is: "*Invictus maneo*". It means, "I remain unconquered".

This is a great motto, for it is the expression of the unconquerable spirit.

It is a motto that any Christian would be glad to adopt.

155

So let's ask what things should not be allowed to conquer us!

We should not be conquered by sorrow and sadness.
No one with any natural feelings can remain untouched by sorrow.

Chrysostom, who was a great preacher in the early Church, used to tell his congregation something worth remembering. He used to urge them not to sorrow overmuch as those who have no hope (1 Thess. 4: 13), but to remember that if they felt sorrow and sadness too much it really meant they had missed the true joy that comes to those who believe Jesus rose again.

Never to feel sorrow would be inhuman, but as Christians we should remember that "beyond the tears lies the glory"; that, because we are Christians, we have very special reasons to be joyful.

Be happy!

Read Acts 25: 1–12.

UNCONQUERED STILL!   Day Four

Here are three more ways in which we should remain "unconquered".

We should not be conquered by disappointment.
Few of you will see all your hopes realised in life and all your dreams come true (though that doesn't mean you shouldn't have them!).

In life we so often meet people who are bitter and resentful because they have not attained the heights they feel they ought to have reached. But to be bitter about this is wrong. Remember St. Paul said he had learned to be "content" in whatever circumstances he was. He accepted the limitations of life.

If you cannot have all your dreams, you must make

156

something good out of what life has given you. In other words, always be *positive* about life!

We should not be conquered by despair.

There is an "ascription of praise" in the book of Revelation (1: 5, 6). It goes like this: "Unto Him that loved us and washed us from our sins in his own blood, and hath made us kings and priests unto God and His Father, to Him be glory and dominion for ever and ever."

Note how often it says *to Him*. At that time the world was giving honour and glory and power to Domitian, the Roman Emperor. At that time the might of Rome was all out to crush the Christian Church. So men generally said "Glory to the Emperor of Rome". But the Christians, even in the midst of persecution, knew that in the end they must give their honour and praise to Jesus. And though this was dangerous and costly, they never gave way to despair over it.

We should not be conquered by temptation.

That is something which is difficult to do—by ourselves. If we face life all alone, temptation both from outside and from within our own hearts will just be too much for us. But if we face life with a sense of the presence and understanding of Jesus, if we walk life with him, if *his* Spirit is within *our* hearts, then we have a "shield of faith" which can "quench all the fiery darts of the wicked one" (Eph. 6: 16), as Paul says.

If we walk alone, we shall stumble and fall.
If we walk with Christ, we remain unconquered.

Read Ephesians 6: 10–24.

THROUGH   Day Five

The *Hamiltons* are one of the greatest of all Scottish families. The Duke of Hamilton is what is called the premier

157

peer of Scotland. He is hereditary keeper of Holyrood-house which is the royal palace of Scotland. He is the peer who had the first vote in the Scottish Parliament, and who had the privilege of leading the vanguard of the Scots in battle.

The Hamiltons, like the Cummings, have a motto of one word: *"Through"*.

It is a magnificent motto.

It is our Christian duty to think things through, that is to try to make up our minds on what is important in life.

Long ago, Plato said that "the unexamined life was the life not worth living". It is necessary for you, as you grow older, to think about all you believe.

"Prove all things," said Paul, "and hold fast that which is good" (1 Thess. 5: 21).

If our faith isn't very important to us; if we only think of it as something learned (as we say) at second-hand; if we have never made any attempt to think out our beliefs and to think them through, then our faith just won't stand up to times of testing if and when they come.

It is also a Christian duty to see things through.

During the last war there was a boy-cyclist messenger in Bristol called Derek Belfall. He was sent with a message when a raid was threatening. He was almost at the post to which he was to deliver his message when a bomb fell. He was blown from his bicycle and mortally wounded.

When the men from the post came to help him, he was barely conscious. But he made a great effort and held out the message he had been given to deliver.

"Messenger Belfall reporting," he whispered. "I have delivered my message."

Do you remember what Jesus said? He said this, "I have finished the work which thou gavest me to do" (John 17: 4).

To see things through, as Derek did and as Jesus did is a wonderful achievement.

Read St. John 17: 1–11.

COURAGE

The *Cumming* family trace their ancestry all the way back to Robert de Comyn who came to this country with William the Conqueror in 1066.

Their motto has only one word in it. It is "Courage".

Courage is a virtue that everyone admires.

Quentin Reynolds, who was a famous American journalist and broadcaster, told, in a war book, about something he saw in London during the days of the last war.

He was walking down a London street. On the other side of the street a commissionaire was standing in a doorway. He was not very young. In those war-time days clothes sometimes looked old, and his uniform was not very tidy or new.

As Quentin Reynolds watched, an army officer came down the road. As he passed the old commissionaire, his arm swung to the salute and he passed on.

Now, why did that happen? Mr. Reynolds wondered why this officer should salute that old commissionaire.

As he was thinking about this, a high-ranking Royal Air Force officer passed. As *he* passed, he too saluted in the direction of the old commissionaire.

Mr. Reynolds was completely mystified, but more was to happen! There came down the street nothing less than a General. As he passed the old commissionaire, he, too, gave him a salute.

Mr. Reynolds felt he had to find out what was happening. He crossed the road to have a closer look at the commissionaire.

As he came closer to him, he suddenly caught sight of

159

something. On the left of the old man's tunic there was a dark red ribbon. It was in fact the ribbon of the Victoria Cross, the highest of all awards for gallantry.

When anyone wears that ribbon, the highest ranking officer in any of the services *must* salute it.

The Victoria Cross is the sign of great courage.
So it, rightly, demands the admiration of all.
Courage is a great virtue, isn't it?

Read Judges 6: 11–24.

TRY!   **Day Seven**

The *Dundases* originally came from the country south of the Forth around Dunbar.
Their motto is one French word: *Essayez!* It means: "Try!"

This is a really great motto. It is something which Jesus would want all his followers to use—*and* put into action.

There are two kinds of people in the world. There are those who say, "It's hopeless"; and there are those who say, "I'll try."

When you read the stories of the miracles which Jesus did, you can see that it was the man who was prepared to try who was helped in the miracles of healing.
For example, Jesus said to the paralysed man whose friends carried him in his presence: "Take up your bed and walk" (Mark 2: 11). The man might well have answered, "That is precisely what it is hopeless for me to try to do." But he tried it. The miracle happened!

Jesus said to the man with the withered hand, "Stretch
160

out your hand" (Mark 3: 5). The man could have said, "Can't you see that it is hopeless for me to try to do that?" But he tried it. The miracle happened!

There is nothing which is so depressing and useless as saying, "It's hopeless."

If we *try*, we can do so much.

And, of course, if we ask Jesus to help us *try*, so much more becomes possible.

Keep trying!

Read St. Mark 3: 1–6.

TRY AGAIN! Day Eight

"*Men are divided into those who say, 'It's impossible', and those who say, 'If you tell me to, I'll try*'," we said yesterday.

There is one matter in which it has been proved true that things can happen if we have faith and trust.

One of the most astonishing things that Jesus ever said to his men was this, "Ye shall be witnesses unto me both in Jerusalem, and in all Judea, and in Samaria, and unto the uttermost parts of the earth" (Acts 1: 8). "Go ye and teach all nations" (Matt. 28: 19). How many were available for this massive operation? There were about one hundred and twenty of them (Acts 1: 15).

If ever it would have been justified to say, "It's impossible", it would have been so for these men. A command to one hundred and twenty uneducated Jews to conquer the world for Jesus looks like insanity.

But they tried! They conquered!

Once when the disciples had toiled all night long at fishing and caught nothing, Jesus told them to let down their nets again. Peter answered rather angrily that they had toiled all night without any success, and he could not see how things could be any better now! "Nevertheless," he said, "at Thy word I will let down the net" (Luke 5: 1–11). The miracle happened!

Miracles happen when you try!
It's worth the risk!
In fact we wouldn't be Christians today unless the first disciples had done just that!

Read Judges 7: 1–8.

GLORY AND VIRTUE   Day Nine

The *Robertsons* came originally from the Atholl country. No family was ever more faithful to the Stewarts and to Bonnie Prince Charlie than they were.

Later their home was in the Rannoch country, at Dunalastair in the shadow of Schiehallion. (The Duncans, incidentally, are part of the Robertson clan and share their tartan, so my editor will be pleased!)

Their motto is a Latin phrase: *Virtutis gloria merces*, which means, "Glory is the reward of virtue".

This really is a great truth. The only way to glory is the way of honour, of honesty and of virtue.

In fact glory is always the result of sheer hard toil!

The Duke of Wellington was once told that Napoleon jeered at him because the word "duty" appeared so often in his despatches, but the word "glory" never. Said the Duke, "The foolish fellow does not see that even if my aim had been glory, the way to it must be duty."

To achieve glory in any sphere of life, you have to work for it.

The great musician or the great singer only gets his

162

"glory" through endless practice, perhaps for many hours a day, *every* day.

The great writer or the great orator only gets "glory" by toil and self-discipline.

The great athlete breaks records only through training and hard work.

There is no easy way to glory.

"The gods," said Hesiod, "have ordained sweat as the price of all things precious."

"I can only promise you blood and sweat and tears and toil," said Sir Winston Churchill in 1940 to Britain faced by the Nazi threat of invasion.

Glory comes the hard way.

Through sheer effort!

Read Judges 11: 29–40.

FOR THE KING   Day Ten

The *Macfies* or *Macphees* originally came from the island of Colonsay, a small island off Western Scotland. Their motto is *Pro Rege*. It means "For the King".

This is the motto of loyalty, of men who will never betray their king.

One of the great stories of loyalty is the story of the eight men of Glenmoriston.

It was in 1746, after the Duke of Cumberland had wiped out the armies of Prince Charlie at the Battle of Culloden. The prince had escaped. He was wandering about in rags, with only one companion.

The government had put a price on his head. They had offered the sum of £30,000 for him, dead or alive.

He came to Glenmoriston cold, miserable and starving. He saw smoke coming from a hut, so he determined to go there, even although there might be enemies there, for anything was better than slow death by starvation.

In the hut there were eight men, two Macdonalds, three Chisholms, one Macgregor, one Grant and one Macmillan. They were all thieves and criminals, and had taken to the hills to escape justice.

When the Prince entered, one of them recognised him, but did not let it be seen that he had done so. The others had to be told, and, when they were told, these eight Highland outlaws guarded, protected and cared for the Prince for weeks.

There was £30,000 on his head, but not one of these men was prepared to be a Judas, and betray him.

They even made a journey to Fort Augustus at the peril of their lives and freedom to buy the Prince a pennyworth of ginger-bread!

It is something of this kind of loyalty that we are all asked to give to Jesus, the Prince of Peace.

Read Daniel 3: 13–30.

LOYALTY   Day Eleven

To continue yesterday's story about Prince Charlie—for weeks the Prince sheltered with the men in Glenmoriston. When he left, he shook hands with each of them.

The years passed by, and the time came when men in Scotland forgot danger and looked back on what was called "the Jacobite rebellion" as a very "romantic" episode, a story of heroism and mystery.

By that time one of the eight men was in Edinburgh. His name was Hugh Chisholm. People would ask him to tell the story of the days when he and his friends had sheltered the Prince in Glenmoriston. He told it with excitement and enthusiasm.

But one thing Hugh Chisholm always did. He always

shook hands with his left hand, for he said *he would never give to any other man the hand that once he had given to his Prince.*

There's loyalty!

It is part of being a disciple to want to serve Jesus with that kind of love and commitment.

It asks a lot of us, but it is the sort of loyalty we ought always to try to give.

Read Daniel 6: 10–23.

NEVER BEHIND! Day Twelve

The *Douglases* take their name from the moorland country in Lanarkshire. Their motto is *Jamais Arrière*, which means, "Never Behind".

There are some things in which the Christian should never be behind! Let's look at these together.

The Christian should never be behind in generosity.
His heart should be the first to feel sorrow and pity for the pain, the sorrow and the want of others. His hand should be the first hand stretched out to help.

That is why we should all be concerned about refugees, the hungry and the homeless.

Dr. A. Rendle Short, in his book *The Bible and Modern Medicine*, points out how the Church has always been in the very forefront of all work to alleviate pain and suffering. Just think on these great facts:

The *first* blind asylum was founded by a Christian monk, Thalasius.

The *first* free dispensary was created by Apollonius, a Christian merchant.

165

The *first* hospital of which there is any record, was founded by a Christian lady called Fabiola.

And there is so much more.

During the great Decian persecution, the Church in Rome had in its care a great crowd of widows, orphans, blind, lame and sick folk.

The heathen prefect broke into the church and demanded that the congregation should hand over its treasures to the State.

Laurentius, the deacon, pointed at the crowd of poor and sick and maimed and lonely and said, "These are the treasures of the Church."

The churches have done so much in the work of caring. In fact, my own church, that is the Church of Scotland, has a magnificent record in this field. It does one of the greatest pieces of social work anywhere, with many Eventide Homes for old people, baby homes, children's homes, places of care for those who drink too much alcohol, for those who get into trouble with the law, for people affected by epilepsy (which is an illness that causes a lot of anxiety and upset), hostels for girls and boys working away from home—and so much more.

And this is true of all the main churches.

So we can be proud of what church people have done to help the suffering.

And you must try when you grow up to play a part in this kind of work.

Read Romans 12: 6–21.

SAY THANKS!   **Day Thirteen**

Here are two more ways in which Christians should never be "behind".

166

The Christian should never be behind in praise.

I once heard a well-known minister say that he had been twenty-five years in a certain church and no one had ever thanked him for a sermon or said that he had enjoyed or been helped by one!

Abraham Lincoln knew human nature, and Abraham Lincoln said, "Everyone likes a compliment."

To give praise and thanks where praise and thanks are due: this can be a wonderfully helpful thing to do in life!

So do it sometimes!

The Christian should never be behind in gratitude.

One of the commonest sins is our failure to say thanks for all the benefits we have received, both from others and from God. To take and never to say thanks is to fail in something very important.

"O give thanks unto the Lord, for he is good," said the Psalmist (Psalm 106: 1).

Don't let's forget to say thanks to God for all his goodness and love.

Christians should never be behind in that!

Read Psalm 107: 1–15.

"DREAD GOD"   Day Fourteen

The *Carnegies* are one of the great Scottish families connected with places called Southesk and Kinnaird. They take their origin from a man called Jocelyn de Ballinhard who lived as long ago as 1203.

Their family motto is "Dread God". It is rather an interesting motto but it is quite a difficult one for you to understand!

This motto speaks to us of the need for reverence.
Do you understand what that word means?

167

The fear of God says the writer of Proverbs, is the beginning of wisdom (Prov. 1: 7). By "beginning" he may well mean not the thing with which wisdom begins, but the chief thing in wisdom. But the point is that the word "fear" shouldn't be taken just as we usually take it. It really means reverence, which is rather like respect!

The philosophers speak to us of what they call the "*numinous*". That rather difficult word describes the feeling of *awe* which comes to all of us at some time or other. It may be you have felt it when you enter a great church, an old cathedral like Canterbury, or a new one like Coventry.
It is the feeling that you are somehow in the presence of something which isn't like anything in the world. It feels more like a "spiritual" thing; you sense that there is something mysterious and "unexplainable" in that place, and that though it feels strange, it is good.
This sort of feeling is something you will understand as you grow older. It is a very important "religious" feeling.

When we are in God's house, we should then behave with reverence, remembering that the place we are in is holy. That was why Moses felt he had to take his shoes off, you remember. He felt he was on holy ground (Ex. 3: 5).
All the great men of the Bible felt this reverence, as Moses did. If you read Isaiah 6, you will find it happens there. Isaiah just felt he was in God's presence and he must "reverence" God.

So "dread God" is an old-fashioned way of saying it. "Dread" just isn't the right word, for it speaks of fear. And the one thing we don't need to have is fear when we think of God! For Jesus told us—and showed us—he is a God of love.

But just because he has loved us so, we should want to show "reverence" to him.

Read Exodus 24: 9–18.

We spoke about the need for reverence yesterday. Let's think of this again in other ways.

The motto "Dread God" speaks to us of the need for obedience.

We do not always take the commands and the demands of God as seriously as we should! We are often tempted to ignore them or to forget them, as if they did not matter very much. They do matter!

When we disobey God, that is when we go *our own way*, we are not so much breaking God's law as we are breaking God's heart. We are being, you might say, rebellious. This hurts God.

One of the things which keeps us from doing many a wrong action is simply the fear of hurting those we love. We find this in connection with our parents for example. We just wouldn't want to hurt them, so we try not to do wrong. If we remembered how our thoughtlessness and our disobedience can hurt God, then we would avoid disobeying him.

It's not a dread of what he can do. It's a feeling of causing sorrow, when it isn't really necessary anyway!

This motto speaks to us of the secret of courage.

If we really reverence God, we shall never really fear any one.

When they buried John Knox, the Earl of Morton looked down. "Here lies one," he said, "who feared God so much that he never feared the face of any man."

To "fear" God is to find the secret of courage. Respect for God makes us bolder and braver.

There is a wrong fear. For example, fear of consequences, fear of the things that men can do, fear of the things that life can do. That kind of fear has no place in our Christian lives.

But there is, too, a right fear, a fear which really means

reverence for God. It is much more fashionable to think sentimentally that God is a good fellow and all will be well.

In fact, reverence for God is the foundation of a right attitude to God, the mainspring of obedience and the secret of that courage which will be with us always.

This reverence for God is the "beginning of wisdom".

Read Exodus 34: 29–35.

NEVER UNPREPARED   Day Sixteen

The *Frasers* come from the Buchan country in the north-east of Scotland and the *Johnstons* come from the Borders.

Their mottoes are almost exactly the same.

One is in French and the other is in Latin.

The motto of the Frasers is *Je suis prest*, which is old French for, "I am ready".

The motto of the Johnstons is *Numquam non paratus*, which is Latin for, "Never unprepared".

Sometimes, a reserve is pitchforked unexpectedly into a team and he seizes his opportunity and plays a wonderful game.

Sometimes an actor or actress who is an understudy has to play the star's part at a moment's notice and scores a personal triumph.

But the success would be quite impossible unless the reserve had trained himself to physical fitness and unless the understudy had memorised and studied the part: otherwise they would not be ready to seize the opportunity when it came.

Study, discipline and preparation are of such tremendous importance when we are young. It is only if you have made yourself ready for it that you can be offered the bigger job when it comes along.

Remember Jesus's example. It was not until he was thirty

years old that he left Nazareth to begin his task (Luke 3: 23).

All that time he had spent in preparation for the great work which God was one day to give him to do.

How well he was prepared for it!

How grateful we are that he was!

Read St. Luke 3: 15–23a.

DON'T FORGET! Day Seventeen

The *Campbells* are one of the best known of Scots families. The Duke of Argyll, with his castle at Inverary, is the head of the clan. He is hereditary Master of Her Majesty's Household, hereditary Lord Justice General, and hereditary Admiral of the Western Coasts and Isles of Scotland, besides being Keeper of the Royal Castles of Dunoon, Carrick, Dunstaffnage and Tarbert.

That sounds impressive, doesn't it?

The *Grahams*, too, coming from the Border areas of Dalkeith and Eskdale, have written their names on Scottish history. Everyone in Scotland knows the names of the Duke of Montrose and John Graham of Claverhouse, the great Jacobite general, who was killed at Killiecrankie!

The Campbells and the Grahams have the same motto, the former in Latin and the other in French.

The motto of the Campbells is *Ne obliviscaris*, and the motto of the Grahams is, *N'oubliez*, both of which mean, "Don't forget".

That is a motto which expresses a duty which all of us must remember. We've got to be like elephants and try never to forget what we should remember.

The famous Ulysses once said that a man is a "part of everything he has met". We are all building memories, and memories are becoming part of what we are.

We shouldn't forget!

We should never forget our debt to the past.

Every generation of people has the benefit of what others have done in the past. We have a great debt to all sorts of people—the man who invented the wheel, for example.

No scientist, doctor or scholar begins at the beginning. He begins where those who lived before him left off. We should be grateful for that.

We receive our civilisation, our liberty, our freedom, a heritage which was bought at a cost—of agony, pain, suffering, work and even the death of those who have gone before us.

That we have freedom to worship in churches, without interference or punishment, is due to the efforts of those who did not have this right easily and fought hard for it.

We have free speech. We can say and think and believe what we like. This is because others struggled to make such freedom possible.

And those of you who are girls will feel that Mrs. Pankhurst, who was chained to railings to draw attention to women's rights, is owed a special debt.

So don't let us forget the past.

We have many blessings from it!

It is our duty to remember those who made life what it is for us. It is our duty to hand on our heritage, not weakened and soiled and tarnished but enhanced.

Read Ecclesiastes 12: 1–7.

GOD NEEDS THE BRAVE   Day Eighteen

The territory of the Buchanans is mainly in Stirlingshire, which is in Central Scotland. The motto of the family is *Audaces iuvo*, that is, "I help the brave".

I suppose that we might say this in the way the proverb says it: "Fortune favours the brave".

Brave people are always needed. God needs brave people. There are certain special ways in which the brave are specially needed in Jesus's work.

The Church needs those who are brave in action.

Robert Louis Stevenson's advice to a young man was, "Stop saying 'Amen' to what the world says, and keep your soul alive."

The most difficult thing in life is to be different. The easy thing is to be a "yes-man", to go with the crowd.

The Church and the world need those who are brave enough, when it is necessary, to defy public opinion, to go against the stream, to be different from the crowd, to have the courage to follow the voice of conscience, the demand of principle, and the summons of God: to be in fact non-conformist.

It is easy to conform, but sometimes God wants us to be non-conformists! We mustn't just do what everybody else is doing without thinking about it. We may need to "stand up" for Jesus.

The Church needs those who are brave in thought, and who are brave enough to express their thoughts.

It needs courage to follow and state the truth. It is very much easier to go on repeating old slogans, to go on reciting old creeds, to go on using old-fashioned language when we should be bold and even revolutionary.

Jesus once said to the disciple John who was concerned about Peter, "What is that to you? Follow me." In other words he was just saying that we all have to be ready to take our own stand.

Will you?

Read Acts 13: 42–52.

173

The Brodies are originally a north-east Scots family, who came from around Nairn on the Moray Firth. Their motto is one word: "Unite!".

It is a magnificent motto.

For unity is strength—always.

Let's think together of parts of life in which unity is important.

First, *in our families*.

William Soutar, the Scottish poet about whom I have already talked, had a gift for what are called "epigrams". These are short sayings, but they have a sting in the tail! Here is one: "A ruined world is rebuilt with hearth-stones." This means that the only thing which can give our lives and our times real security and stability is the home.

One of the things I hope you will do as you grow older is to build Christian homes in which old and young, parents and children, this generation and the previous generation, are not divided in misunderstanding but are united in real friendship, fellowship and love, where the old and young have not drifted apart (as seems so common nowadays), but are together.

We hear a lot about the "problem" of juvenile delinquency, as older people call it! The cure for that problem is not changing the law, not creating a better educational system (though that might help)—it is in the home.

Where the home is secure and loving, you won't find juvenile delinquency.

From unity in our homes let's think about church unity.

At a time when church union is talked about so much, we sometimes ask with shame, "How can we expect union between different branches of the Church, when so many congregations in *every* church are torn and rent in two, and when every one of the churches is itself divided into differing sects and parties?"

Where there is bitterness, strife, hatred, envy, discord, the work of Christ can never be done. God's greatest gift to his Church is to have in it those who sow peace.

Satan's greatest allies are those who sow strife.

I hope you will all do what you can for church unity.

Jesus is not divided!

Read Acts 1: 12–26.

DIVISION IN THE NATION — Day Twenty

Unity is important somewhere else—*in the nation*!

Bit by bit the old class distinctions which divided men are being broken down. This is good. There are few places today where the old feudal distinctions between, for example, a master and a servant still hold good.

I have been at more than one function at which the Provost of the Burgh (or as they say in England, the Mayor), who occupied the place of honour, was an ordinary workman in a public works, and at which one or more of the guests was a managing director of the same works! That is good and right!

But one of the great national problems today is that time and time again one section, one trade, one set of craftsmen in the community, demands for itself rights and privileges at the expense of the whole community. And so, all too often, each section is indifferent to the result of its demands upon other sections of the community.

Selfishness, in individuals, is wrong because it hurts others.

Selfishness and self-interest can equally hurt the life of our community or our country.

There must be unity in the world.

Nowadays you would not expect some people to talk of

175

the possibility of war any more than normal people would talk about the possibility of suicide. War is madness now, more than it ever has been.

I don't really know how any Christian can be other than against all war. It is absolutely impossible to imagine any circumstances under which Jesus Christ would approve the use of nuclear weapons.

So the world today faces the simple alternative of unity or destruction.

Unity in our homes comes when Jesus is the unseen but ever remembered guest in our house.

Unity in the Church can only come when the Church ceases to be the Church of Scotland or the Church of England or any other Church and becomes simply the Church of Jesus Christ.

Unity in the nation can only come when men set Christian duty and Christian responsibility above party or selfish interest.

Unity in the world can only come when "the kingdoms of the world" become "the kingdoms of the Lord and of his Christ", as our Bible says.

Unite!

Read Isaiah 5: 1–10.

PRAY AND WORK   Day Twenty-one

Ramsay is the clan or family name of the Earl of Dalhousie, who is the head of one of the most ancient and famous Scottish families. The motto of the Ramsays is the Latin phrase *Ora et Labora*, which means, "Pray and Work".

Prayer and work are very closely connected, because we should not treat our prayers as if they were a way to get something without working for it.
To prayer must always be added work and effort and toil.

176

We must not think that all we have to do is to pray for something, then it will fall into our hands. It is wrong to look on God as an easy way out, or to look on God as the person who will do for us what we are too lazy to do for ourselves!

Long ago the ancient philosopher Epicurus said, "It is vain to ask of the gods what a man is capable of supplying for himself."

This is what we were taught in the Lord's Prayer. Jesus taught us to pray, "Give us this day our daily bread." But we cannot just pray, then sit back and wait for our daily bread to fall into our hands! We have to work for it and work hard; we have to sow the seed, till the ground, harvest the crop, grind the corn, prepare the food, before we can actually have our daily bread.

James, in his Epistle, said that "faith without works" is useless!

So, really, is prayer without work.

Don't you agree?

Read James 2: 14–26.

SERVICE IS THE MOTTO   Day Twenty-two

Many of you will have travelled in a plane! That used to be a very special experience, but now an aeroplane is just a normal, convenient "vehicle" for getting quickly from place to place.

I must confess, however, that a journey by air is for me a great thrill. It is also something which I still approach with trepidation!

I remember once being on my way to Germany by plane. British European Airways (as they were then called) give their passengers an excellent little handbook of information

177

and maps. One sentence in that book seemed to me a great ideal. "We have a motto," I read, "and it goes like this: 'Our passengers are the purpose of our business—not an interruption in our work, and we shall try in every way to live up to it'."

Another thing the booklet said was, "The bell at the side of your seat will bring your steward or stewardess to you. You have only to ask. Their job is to make your flight comfortable and pleasant." So the stewards and stewardesses don't look on a request for help as an interruption or a nuisance. It is something they are there to carry out. To serve the passengers and satisfy their needs is their responsibility.

Big business is built on nothing less than the Christian ideal of service! The more it fulfils that ideal, the more successful it is.

A certain writer tells of a shoe firm whose advertisement read, "We are at your feet!" And he mentions an automobile service-station whose only claim was, "We are prepared to crawl under your car oftener and to get ourselves dirtier than any of our competitors."

Their job was service!

It is so easy to regard people as a nuisance!

But this is something we must not do!

For it is something Jesus never did!

And God never does.

Read St. Luke 4: 40–44.

KNOCK HERE!   Day Twenty-three

Kermit Eby, who was a great American teacher, tells how he made it a rule always to be available to his pupils and students. The door to his house was always open. And so he was always ready to help.

"I know," he says, "that research is important; I also know that a man is more important than a footnote."

Nobody was an interruption or a nuisance to him.

A Salvation Army writer tells of a certain Mrs. Berwick who retired from active work with the Army in Liverpool. She had been engaged for years on social work, and she came to spend her old age in London.

The War came with its terrible air-raids. People somehow or other got the idea that her house was safe.

She was old, but the experience of her Liverpool days had never left her. Her instinct was to bind up wounds and do what she could for everyone whom she saw was suffering. So she assembled a simple first-aid box, and she put a notice in her window. It said, "If you need help, knock here."

Wasn't that a marvellous example from that very wonderful lady?

How good it will be if throughout *your* lives, you are known as people who help—always.

Read St. Luke 18: 1–8.

READY TO HELP   Day Twenty-four

We have been thinking about people who were always willing to help.

Here is someone else!

William Corbett Roberts was a rather unusual but very loved rector of St. George's, Bloomsbury, in London.

A stranger, looking for some information one day, had to leave a message for Corbett Roberts with one of the church cleaners.

He said, "I hardly like to trouble him."

Back came the cleaner's answer, "Nothing's a trouble to *our* rector."

That *was* a compliment!

When we are very busy on some urgent matter, when we are comfortably settled down to watch TV, when we have some plan of our own we want to work out, it is so easy to think of someone who comes asking for our help as a nuisance, isn't it?

Let's say it again.

Jesus was not like that.

Luke tells how Jesus tried to get away from the crowds. He took his disciples into a desert place to be alone, but the crowds chased after him with all their needs and troubles. He might so easily have told them that *He* must have *His* quiet time, *His* rest, *His* prayer, *His* preparation.

He didn't.

He was ready to help, because he felt compassion and love for them.

"He received them and spake unto them of the Kingdom of Heaven, and healed them that had need of healing" (Luke 9: 10, 11).

No one can be like Jesus and find someone in need an interruption or a nuisance.

Let your love be like that of Jesus!

Read St. Luke 9: 10–17.

REMEMBER!   **Day Twenty-five**

Harry Emerson Fosdick, a great American preacher, tells a story about a boy who was living a bad life, and was studying biology.

One day he was shown, under the microscope, the life of little creatures which are born and breed and die all within a matter of minutes.

He, *literally*, saw generations of these microscopic creatures rise and pass away before his eyes. It made him think of the value of life, and he suddenly said, "I resolve, God helping me, never to be a weak link in the chain."

We said earlier that we must remember our debt to the past. We must also remember our duty to the future. This means we must remember our teachers, our parents, our Church, and all the good that people have sacrificed to make us what we are.

Here is something else and someone else we should never forget.

We should never forget Jesus Christ and all he has done for us.

Jesus knew how easily we forget, so he gave us his "sacrament" to help us. You remember how we said we should take bread and wine and remember. He said, "This do *in remembrance* of me" (Luke 22: 19). So when we go to church and share the sacrament, everyone knows it is an act of remembering Jesus Christ.

Yes, we must remember!

Read St. Luke 22: 7–23.

ONE WORD   Day Twenty-six

Here are several words all closely related, but all with very different meanings.

There is *fame*.
There is *notoriety*.
There is *glory*.

They all imply that there is something *outstanding* (good or bad!) about the person to whom they are ascribed.

181

To be *notorious* is to be known for things which are not very praiseworthy.

To be *famous* is to be known for great things, of whatever kind.

To have *glory* is always to be known for good.

Sometimes the Bible has a way of summing up a man in one sentence. It says of Nadah, king of Israel, in one sentence, "He did evil in the sight of the Lord" (1 Kings 15: 26).

It is curious how we sum people up in one word. When someone dies, he leaves a memory which is often summarised in one word! Some will say of him that he was "sarcastic", that he was "unreliable", that he was "kind". But always, for good or for bad, there is that one word verdict!

What do you consider people say—or think—of you?

It doesn't really matter what people think of us so long as *we* know that what *we* are doing is right and good. But it is rather nice to think, too, that if people do sum us up in a word, it is a *good* word they choose!

Read Psalm 1.

THE BOAT HOME   Day Twenty-seven

A Scottish lady emigrated to America with her family. She was not very happy in the United States.

When she was first in America, before she had settled down, she used to grumble a lot and regret having crossed the Atlantic. When she got into one of these moods her husband used always to say to her:

"Well, there's a boat home!"

That phrase became a kind of catch-word in that household!

That lady and her husband later had children. The children, though never allowed to forget their Scots ancestry, grew up as Americans.

When the daughter of the family was still only a little girl, a British visitor came to the house, who rather discourteously criticised American politics, in general, and President Eisenhower, who was then President, in particular.

The little girl could stand it no longer. She turned to the critical visitor and out came the family catchword, "Well, if you don't like it, there's a boat home!"

I'm afraid the little girl was immediately sent away from the table. Afterwards her father told her that while he quite agreed with her, children did not talk that way to grown-ups!

Still the child's remark was effective!

The critical visitor said no more.

"If you don't like it, leave it!" That is good advice.

Admittedly, it is not always possible to do this. There are times when we have to stick things out whether we like them or not. But there are also times when we can, if we wish, "take the boat home" at any time.

If we are for ever grumbling about our friends, the place where we stay, the things we do, then let's not just criticise, but try to do something about it. If the club we go to isn't happy, rather than just criticise, find a better one.

Grumblers can be very tiresome!
There is a boat home!

Read St. Matthew 22: 1–14.

ALL-ROUNDER   Day Twenty-eight

I once saw an advertisement which amused me and made me think. It was on behalf of a firm of painters and decorators. It said this: "Specialists in all kinds of painting and decorating".

183

At first that seemed quite ridiculous! To claim to be an expert in everything was just too much for me! In fact to say you are an expert in *everything* seems to me to be saying two contradictory things! If you are an expert, you must be a specialist in something; but it just can't be everything.

If we go to a "medical" specialist, we go to someone who is *an expert* on some particular part of the body, like the heart or the lungs, the ear or the throat at the most.

In stamp-collecting, a specialist is a man who has studied the stamps of one particular country, or perhaps the stamps of one particular issue of one country.

We do not expect a musician to be a specialist on every instrument.

Would it be likely that someone who was an expert on the piano would also be an expert trumpeter?

Or a violinist play the trombone?

It can happen, but it's not likely.

In sport we do not expect a cricketer to be a specialist in batting, bowling and wicket-keeping. He specialises in one branch of the game.

We do not expect an expert goal-keeper to be an equally expert striker in football, do we?

So really the idea of a universal specialist sounds rather funny. A man can be (as they say) "Jack of all trades and master of none".

But there is another side to this. We speak of the *all-rounder*, and a very useful person the all-rounder is. He can bat well enough, and he can take his turn with the ball, and if need be he can take the pads and the gloves and keep wicket.

In the football team the all-rounder can play a good game in any position. There have been exceptional people who represented their country at cricket, tennis, *and* golf. Yes, all three!

Even in medicine we have the general practitioner (that is

the ordinary doctor), who is expert enough to recognise most of the things that are wrong with us.

So while it is unusual to find experts in everything, you will be very useful to people if you can do a lot of things well.

So don't despise the all-rounder!

He (or she) can be a very useful person to have around.

Read St. John 1: 35–51.

INGRATITUDE   Day Twenty-nine

A certain man came to Tertullian, the Roman writer, with a problem: the difficulty of earning a living in a heathen world.

What should the Christian mason do if he was asked to build a heathen temple?

What should the Christian tailor do if he was asked to make clothes for a heathen priest?

What should the Christian soldier do if he is ordered to burn his incense on the altar in the camp?

Tertullian obviously said he must be devout to his faith.

So the man finished up by saying, "But I must live."

Tertullian answered, "Must you?"

If it comes to a choice between our Christian principles and our job, work, or our popularity, what would *we* do?

Are we prepared to take a risk for our Christian faith?

When people look for security they tend to look for it in the wrong place.

They seek for it by taking precautions, of a worldly kind—like the insurance we spoke about in Month 2, Day 6.

But there is a safety far beyond that, and it is that safety that matters.

In the 1914–18 War Rupert Brooke wrote his poem *Safety*.

> Safe shall be my going
>   Secretly armed against
>   all death's endeavour;
> Safe though all safety's lost;
>   safe when men fall;
> And if these poor limbs die,
>   safest of all.

A Roman Catholic cardinal threatened Martin Luther, the great Protestant reformer, with all kinds of vengeance. He told him that his present supporters would soon leave him in the lurch.

"Where will *you* be then?" he demanded menacingly.

"Then as now," said Luther, "then as now—in the hands of God."

This is the security that really matters!
As the old hymn has it, "Safe in the arms of Jesus."

Truly underneath are the everlasting arms!

Read Deuteronomy 33: 26–29.

TAKE AIM! Day Thirty

We need something to aim at in life.

When we are going on a long journey in a motor-car, we carry a map and study the route, and we say, "We'll get to such and such a place by tonight, and we'll spend the night there."

We are so confident that we shall get there that we book rooms in a hotel there before we start on our journey!

When one of you is studying, you know that you must get to a certain stage in time for the examination. You must get to that chapter, that theorem, that section in the book, that line of the text.

Even in sport you set yourself a certain standard. You set yourself a figure and you make up your mind to reach it—whether it's a four-minute mile or a low handicap at golf.

In every part of life we set ourselves an aim and a goal. But strangely enough, we don't always do that in the business of life itself.

We would all do much better and achieve much more if we deliberately set ourselves to gain a new virtue and to lose an old fault.

"I press toward the mark", said St. Paul (Phil. 3: 14).

And the mark for him—the prize of the high calling of God in Jesus. It's a great aim.

We also need someone to help us in living.

The great American preacher, Dr. Harry Emerson Fosdick, has a sermon, the title of which I have always remembered. It is "No man need stay the way he is."

If our Christian faith means anything to us, that phrase is true. Jesus's power can help us to go farther and farther along the road to holiness, if we will ask for the help which he offers to us, and receive it with joy.

"I press toward the mark," said St. Paul. Yes, it's worth repeating that great phrase.

It is not enough for a Christian to accept a life which is "stuck" in the one place.

Life should be the road to holiness, an upward and an onward way.

Keep going on . . . and up!

Read Proverbs 4: 7–12.

187

MONTH SIX

I am recovering from an attack of speechlessness!

I lost my voice completely and I could only speak to the outside world in a hoarse whisper. My voice failed me quite suddenly in the middle of a day's work.

On the way home I thought it would be a good idea if I called in at a chemist's shop and bought a gargle. So I did.

I explained, as best I could with hand signs, to the girl behind the counter what I wanted. I didn't need to tell her that I had lost my voice! She recommended what she thought would help most.

As she wrapped up the bottle and handed it to me across the counter and took my money, she smiled and said, "You must have been talking too much!"

She was more right than she knew, and correct in a far deeper way than she intended, because the trouble with us all is that we talk too much!

Torrents of words flood this world of ours. Oceans of good advice are poured out, cataracts of sermons are unleashed.

There is enough Christian talk in this world to reform half a dozen worlds!

The trouble is that, for all the talk, there is so little action. And it is the action that matters in the end.

Jesus said, "By their fruits ye shall know them. Not everyone that *saith* unto me, Lord, Lord, shall enter into the kingdom of heaven; but he that doeth the will of my Father which is in heaven" (Matt. 7: 20, 21).

When Jesus painted a picture of God as judge, the standard was simply whether or not a man had been kind (Matt. 25: 31–46).

James (whose letter had the ill-fortune to be called by Martin Luther "a right strawy epistle") nevertheless laid it down, "Pure religion and undefiled before God and the Father is this, to visit the fatherless and the widows in their

affliction, and to keep himself unspotted from the world"
(James 1: 27).

I believe he was right.

Read Isaiah 53: 1–10.

TO ACTION STATIONS! Day Two

Thomas Chalmers was one of Scotland's chief orators.
After a great speech, he was congratulated by all his friends.
"Yes," he answered, "but *what did it do?*"

Had the words simply (as we say) gone whistling down
the wind?

The Church is littered with discussion groups—and
discussion groups can be intensely valuable, but *they are
not valuable if people are only sitting and talking when they
ought to be acting*, and if action does not follow the
discussion.

Florence Allshorn was one of the great missionary
teachers. She was principal of a women's missionary college.
She was always annoyed by the type of person who suddenly
discovered that her quiet time for prayer was due just when
the dirty dishes were waiting to be washed in the kitchen!

To discuss or pray is rather pointless when help round
the house is really what is required.

Robert Louis Stevenson once turned on someone, who
expressed the highest sentiments but did nothing, with the
words, "I cannot hear what you say for listening to what
you are."

People will remember your kindness in a time of trouble
when they have forgotten every word you have used.

"Faith without works is dead," says that book of James.
It is.

Take up *your* action stations!

Read Haggai 1: 1–15.

A minister whom I knew joined the Royal Navy in the First World War. He was a big man, easily the biggest in his squad, so he soon found himself with the nickname "Lofty".

In charge of the squad there was a cockney petty officer from London, who was also a champion Navy boxer. He was a small man, and he wanted some special boxing practice before a certain tournament.

My friend thought that Lofty was the very man to give him some practice. The fact that Lofty was so big and he was so small would only make the practice more useful!

He asked my friend if he would put on the gloves with him. The latter said he had never boxed in his life, but he would try it if he liked. So he put on the gloves, and the petty officer told him to bore in and try to hit him.

Lofty bore in all right, but left himself wide open. The petty officer stopped him, and told him to cover up his chin, or he might get hurt.

They started again. This time Lofty's wide-open chin was too much of a temptation for the cockney champion. He hit out so hard that Lofty fell to the ground. But he jumped up ruefully rubbing his chin.

The little petty officer stopped him. "Lofty," he said, "if ever you're boxing, remember one thing—and don't forget it. Don't ever let your opponent see that you're hurt."

It is good advice for a boxer.
But it is good advice to you and me too.

To let people see that you have been hurt can be a weakness.

It is much better to "keep a stiff upper lip" and battle on: to grin and bear it, and fight on.

Keep fighting. St. Paul did, even under arrest.

Read Acts 28: 23–31.

The world often seems to be full of people who are always getting hurt *and* telling the world about it!

Sometimes your friends will say they are "not going to play any more"—just because they can't win, perhaps!

Church members find things are done in a way they don't think they should be done, so they become regular grumblers and grousers in the church.

A junior choir member doesn't get the solo he or she thinks was due—so he goes off in a huff!

Someone is not thanked for what he has done. It's a tragedy! The whole community hears about it!

Someone is not invited to join the "platform party" or be up front! The whole world hears about that!

It is a good phrase that tells us "to grin and bear it". It is good advice.

In *sport*, we admire the player who can take a knock and bounce up smiling.

In *business*, we admire the man who can take a failure or a disappointment and come back still smiling and still fighting.

Do you remember how Kipling has it:

> If you can meet with Triumph and Disaster
> And treat these two impostors just the same.

Then he goes on:

> If you can make one heap of all your winnings
> And risk it on one turn of pitch-and-toss
> And lose, and start again at your beginnings
> And never breathe a word about your loss.

The ability to get up and fight back was to Kipling the sign of a real man—as it is of a real woman.

Read Acts 12: 1–17.

194

The greatest of all the Greek kings was Alexander the Great, the man who, before he was thirty, wept because there were no more worlds left to conquer.

One of the most interesting stories about Alexander comes from his Persian campaigns.

He had put Darius into a position in which defeat was certain. Darius realised this and offered Alexander terms which were very favourable: a great ransom for the captives which had been taken, a mutual alliance, and the hand of one of his daughters in marriage.

Darius offered all this if only Alexander would halt, stay his hand and be content with that which he had won. Alexander told Parmenio, his chief of staff, of the terms which had been offered.

Parmenio said, "If I were you, I would accept them."

Alexander replied, "So would I—if I were Parmenio."

Alexander was Alexander! For him there was nothing less than absolute victory!

A lesser man would be content with lesser things. But for Alexander it was all or nothing!

It is interesting to see how great men have always had a sense of their own greatness.

Napoleon's plans and schemes had led him into conflict with the Pope.

He had an uncle who was a cardinal. The uncle protested against Napoleon's actions, and warned him to be content with less. The uncle was an old man and had poor eyesight.

It was night time. Napoleon took him to the window and pointed into the night. "Do you see that star?" he asked. The poor-sighted old cardinal answered, "No, sir."

Napoleon answered, "But I see it; you may go."

Napoleon could see the star.
The cardinal just couldn't.
Do you get the point?

It doesn't of course mean that, because of this, Napoleon was one of the heroes of history. What it does mean is that great men and women often see a vision and a possibility far beyond what ordinary men and women see.

Greatness comes from seeing and following that vision.

Read St. Matthew 2: 1–12.

DO YOU FEEL GREAT? Day Six

When Admiral Sir A. B. Cunningham was a schoolboy twelve years old, he went to stay in Ireland. His father, a world famous surgeon, wished to get the boy's future settled, and a chance arose to get the lad into the Navy. He sent the boy a telegram saying, "Would you like to join the Royal Navy?"

The boy immediately wired back, "Yes, would very much like to be an admiral."

To be great you must have a *sense* of greatness. This is not conceit. It is just realising your own ability to tackle a big job.

How do you acquire that sense of greatness?

The first answer is that it comes from self-respect.

When Nehemiah was urged to seek safety in the hour of his danger, his answer was, "Should such a man as I flee?" (Neh. 6: 11). This is one of the seeds of greatness.

Many a man and many a woman have been compelled to be great, because they respected themselves and would not let themselves down.

It's a spur to greatness to have respect for yourself.

The second answer comes from the fact that others are thinking of us, hoping for us, believing in us, praying for us.

George Washington once said, "I shall not despair so long as I know that one faithful saint is praying for me."

You carry on you, and in you, the hopes and the dreams

196

of those to whom you are dear—parents, teachers, friends. This will help you to be greater, because you won't want to let them down.

The third help is the knowledge that God is behind us.

Every time we say goodbye, and every time we use the word "goodbye", we are saying the words, "God be with you!" In other words we tell people to go in the strength of the Lord.

The world needs men and women who can think greatly and act greatly.

These three things may help *you* to feel great!

Read Nehemiah 6: 10–16.

STAY YOUNG!   Day Seven

"His activity was inexhaustible, his interest universal. Into each month of his life he crammed a year. He laughed at time and distance. To preach in his own church, teach in the Sunday School, carve the joint, try out a new pony, visit the cook's declining father, walk six miles each way to preach in another church, return to miscalculate his accounts and dictate his diary—this was just an average Sunday to him.

"And at seventy he is setting out to emigrate to Canada to see what it is like!"

Who was this youthful seventy-year old? The grandfather of R. C. Robertson-Glasgow, the well-known writer.

But listen to this!

John Wesley says that when he was eighty-six he found it difficult to preach more than twice a day!

And what of the story of a very much alive lady—a really great lady—who told me that she could not afford time in

197

hospital for a minor operation because she had only ten more working years and she was so busy directing a clinic and running groups? She was eighty-seven when she said that!

Age has very little to do with the date which happens to be entered on our birth certificates. Sometimes boys and girls seem to be much older than their years, too.

Some people are never really young.

Like the boy on whose annual report his headmaster wrote: "Would make an excellent father." Others never really grow old. "They have never grown up," we say. And that can be quite a good thing.

There is a very ancient proverb. It goes, "Whom the gods love die young." It does not mean that those "whom the gods love" die in their youth or their early years. It means that, if the gods love a man, *no matter what age he is,* he still has the gift of essential youth. He is still young in heart.

How do people stay young?

What keeps you really alive is *interest.* If you want to stay young, be interested in many things.

Find life exciting!

Discover!

The secret of "eternal youth" is *wonder.* So long as you find new things to wonder at, you will never grow old; at least not in heart!

Learn to be interested and stay young!

Read St. John 20: 1–10.

THE WHOLE TRUTH   Day Eight

Have you heard of Fleet Street?

It is, of course, the great "street of newspapers" in London.

In a book called *Faith in Fleet Street*, Robert Moore tells of one of his experiences as a journalist. He was asked to write a special report, and he found he could not get anywhere with it.

This worried him and indeed alarmed him. The investigation had been asked for personally by the great Lord Beaverbrook—who owned the *Daily Express*—because of information given to him by one of his senior editors.

Robert Moore knew that the story was inaccurate, no matter who had passed on the information. Fearfully he went back to his editor and said so.

The editor told him to drop the investigation at once. Then he said something which Robert Moore never forgot, because it was good advice to a journalist. "Anyone who spends his time and energies and his experience fully proving that there is not a story to write has done just as good a day's work as someone who proves that there is a story."

In other words, the paper was not interested in just getting a story. It was interested in the truth.

Robert Moore writes of "the temptations and opportunities for a journalist that are lined up on every bar counter; stacked high in every whisper and gossip, and which sometimes shriek at him on that blank sheet of paper in his typewriter at which he has been staring seemingly for hours."

He says, "I can never, must never, say that my journalism is the truth, the whole truth, and nothing but the truth. But this I do say, that my journalism is the result of looking for the truth."

In the same book T. E. Uttley writes, "The first business of a newspaper is to describe life as it is—remorselessly, accurately, and with fanatical detachment."

Journalists look for the truth. However interesting a story may be, it is not a good story unless it is a true story.

There is a very big lesson for us all in this incident. It is "the truth, the whole truth, and nothing but the truth" that matters in every part of life.

Be true to your standards.
Tell the truth!
Love the truth!

Read Ephesians 4: 7–15.

NOTHING BUT THE TRUTH! Day Nine

Christians should love the truth as much as good journalists honour it. Yet too often the so-called Christian will repeat a story, a rumour, or a piece of gossip.

The good journalist resists the temptation to write sensational stories. Christians sometimes fall into that temptation. I think this is what St. Paul meant when he said (as one version has 1 Corinthians 13), "Love isn't glad when things go wrong for others."

We should never repeat a story if we are uncertain as to its truth.

In war-time we were constantly reminded that "careless talk costs lives." At any time, it can break hearts. We shouldn't do it.

We should never repeat what we have been told by a friend who trusts us.

There is a story told of a lady in France who talked too much. Her priest set her a "penance", which is a form of punishment for a sin. She was to take a dead hen and walk through the country lanes pulling its feathers out and throwing them away.

She found this easy.

"But there is more to it," said the priest. "Now go out again and gather the feathers up."

It was impossible. The winds had blown them far and wide.

"That," said the priest, "is what happens to your careless, harmful words. You utter them freely, but you can never take them back again. The damage is done!"

Watch your careless talk!
There are few things that can do more damage than the tongue!

Read Psalm 119: 33–40.

YOUR GIFTS   Day Ten

I once visited the little village of Glenluce in Wigtownshire in south-west Scotland. There can only be a thousand people in the whole area. The congregation itself has about six hundred members.

A year or two ago the congregation found that their church was in such a dangerous condition that many repairs and much rebuilding was necessary. So they re-designed and reconstructed the whole church! That took £10,000 to do and what impressed and amazed me was that, in no more than two years, the people in that small village raised the money! It is, to me, one of the most remarkable efforts ever.

How was it done?
First, they set out their aims. They were going to rebuild their church, whatever happened!
Now this was a wise policy. People knew what they were aiming for.
It is so much easier to raise money for something definite than for some vague reason. Everybody knew that the money was going to rebuild that church. So they helped willingly.

The second important thing was that everyone was to

help. This wasn't just a "church" thing. The whole village, whether they went to church or not, wanted the church in the village to be kept safe.

St. Paul knew the value of this sort of thing when he talked about different kinds of "gifts". We all have things *we* can do, he said, so be sure to help.

Nehemiah did just the same when he asked people to help him rebuild the walls of Jerusalem.

You see God needs the help of everyone.

So whatever your gifts, (and you will have a gift of some kind) let God use it!

Read Nehemiah 4: 16–23.

TRUST IN GOD ...   Day Eleven

"In God we trust; all others pay cash."

That was the rather amusing notice a friend of mine saw in a garage recently.

But behind that strange notice there is a great truth.

God is the only completely trustworthy person in the universe.

Let's just think about this.

The Bible writers have a lot of things to say about whom not to trust, about whom we must always be careful of. And, of course, about *what* not to trust.

For example, they warn against trust in *riches*.

Listen to this!

"Put no confidence in extortion; set no vain hopes on robbery; if riches increase, set not your heart on them" (Psalm 62: 10).

Tragic is the fate of the men "who trust in their wealth and boast of the abundance of their riches" (Psalm 49: 6).

The man who "would not make God his refuge, but trusted in the abundance of his riches, and sought refuge in his wealth" is doomed in the end to become the laughing-stock of wiser men (Psalm 52: 7).

"He who trusts in riches will wither," says the Sage, "but the righteous will flourish like a green leaf" (Proverbs 11: 28).

It is foolish to put our trust in something as easily lost as money!

Riches aren't everything!

The Bible writers were impressed by the way in which friends can let us down.

It is the complaint of the Psalmist that "the bosom friend in whom we trusted," the friend who ate bread with him, has turned against him (Psalm 41: 9).

"Put no confidence in a neighbour," says Micah, "have no confidence in a friend" (Micah 7: 5).

It is rather a grim thought, isn't it? But the Psalmist knew life and knew how easily people can let each other down.

So be careful who and what you trust.
But always you can trust God!
He won't let you down!
Ever!

Read Proverbs 3: 5–10.

WATER FROM THE WELL   Day Twelve

We often holiday at a place called Elie, in Fife, Scotland.

In one of our holiday hotels there, two of the staff are husband and wife and we now know them well. They come from a near-by village.

The husband once was taken ill suddenly and seriously. He was removed to an infirmary. His wife visited him daily and naturally we asked how he was getting on.

One night his wife said, "Do you know what he said today?"

I said, "No, do tell me."

"Well," she said, "When I asked him if there was anything

203

I could bring him, he said, 'All I would like is a drink of water from the pump that draws the water from the well in the village street'."

Next day his wife took him a vacuum flask full of water from the village well!

If you know your Bible, you will immediately think of David when he hid in the cave of Adullam. What he wanted above all was a drink of water from the well that was beside the gate (2 Sam. 23: 13–18).

When you are up against it, it is the simple things you want—like water from the village well.

It is my job to teach in a university. I know then how it is to be a scholar. But I sometimes wonder if religion is really as difficult and as complicated as scholars make it out to be. So often it is a simple faith we need.

Joel Carmichael in his book *The Death of Jesus* says that, since the nineteenth century there have been 60,000—yes, 60,000—lives of Jesus written. I have had to read and lecture on many of them, and sometimes I cannot help remembering what my predecessor, that great scholar James Denney, said to an American, when he asked, "Can you recommend a good life of Jesus?" Denney answered, "Have you tried the one Luke wrote?"

Back to the Bible!

Yes, in many ways that is the simple thing to do. The Gospel of St. Mark—or St. Luke—will help us much more in life than the complicated arguments of some wordy theologian.

> Jesus loves me, this I know.
> For the Bible tells me so.

Simple.
But true!

Read 2 Samuel 23: 13–18.

I hope you will be adventurers!

You would not be normal growing boys and girls if you didn't.

But I hope too that you will be ready to listen to the voice of experience.

It is because older people have come to understand dangers in life through their experience that they sometimes do things that seem to hold you back!

Listen to the voice of experience and test what it says.

Shakespeare once said, "Crabbed age and youth cannot live together." I don't know about the "crabbed" part, but I hope it is *not* true that young people and old people can't get on together.

There is a lovely picture of the rather old Peter and the rather young John hurrying to the tomb from which, they had heard, Jesus had risen. It says in the Gospels of them that they ran "both of them together" (John 20: 4).

Youth and age hurrying to see Jesus!

Sometimes experience says "Be careful of starting on drugs, or drink, or even cigarettes. For they can ruin life." You may feel this is just older people being restrictive. "We can look after ourselves," you say. But playing about with drugs isn't really wise, is it? Many young people have found out later that they ought to have listened to the "voice of experience".

When you become a motor driver, you must learn the Highway Code. It is, really, the experience of many drivers put together to help others. That experience is invaluable.

It is the same with life. To think about and learn from older people's experience is not soft. It is sense. And it doesn't stop you being an adventurer in the things that matter.

Read Joshua 8: 30–35.

We were thinking yesterday of the "gap" between young and old. I said I hoped you would always be able and willing to learn from your older friends.

I do.

But it is still true that there will be different points of view between old and young.

An authoress called May Sinclair tells how she said to her small daughter that, when she was a little girl, there were certain things that she was not allowed to do.

"But you must remember, mummy," the little girl said, "you were then and I'm now."

Times change; ways change; so what you must have (and if I dare say it to you!) your parents must have, is an attitude of understanding. They must understand your "now". You must understand their "then"!

I was an only child, but my wife was one of five sisters. I therefore have an assortment of nephews and nieces and grand-nephews and grand-nieces!

In 1968 Mrs. Barclay was in Canada with Jane, our daughter, to visit a sister of hers who lives and works there. Naturally, many photographs were taken. Then in 1969 my sister-in-law came to Scotland to visit her own family and us. So naturally the photographs were on show!

They were being shown to Julie, one of my grand-nieces, who was about three years old. She lives very near us and knows Jane well.

When Julie saw the photograph of Jane and my wife, she said, "Look! That's Jane and her friend!"

Mother and daughter—but to Julie, daughter and friend.

Wouldn't it be wonderful if your parents were able to be called your friends?

We do not really need to have an unbridgeable gap between us and our parents. We should all do that we can to ensure that we and our parents are good, understanding friends.

Read 1 Samuel 16: 19–23.

TO EAT—TO REMEMBER Day Fifteen

I left school in 1925—which must sound like ancient history to you!

Some years ago, because something rather important had happened to one of my old school class-mates, we decided to meet for an evening together.

Since then we have been meeting for one evening each year!

When we are all there, we can muster about fourteen, from all over this country and beyond.

We have two doctors, one medical officer of health, one lawyer, two headmasters, one bank manager, one works manager, one chief accountant of the United States Army, one former Moderator of the General Assembly of the Church of Scotland, and two professors.

That's not a bad roll-call for one class from one school, is it?

When we met again for the first time, it was forty years since some of us had seen each other! Yet we all knew each other immediately. From the very first moment things seemed just as they were years before. Even the old nick-names were flying around!

So that night annually, we eat and drink—and remember.

Does that strike a chord with you?

Can you think of a "meal" that takes place nowadays at which we eat and drink and remember?

"This do—in remembrance," we say.

Of Jesus.

This is exactly what the Lord's Supper or Communion

207

(as some call it) or the Eucharist (as others call it) or the Mass (as, for example, Roman Catholics call it) really is— a remembering of that first meal in an upper room.

So we too eat and drink—and remember.

Read St. Matthew 26: 20–30.

MEMORY, GRATITUDE, LOYALTY   Day Sixteen

The people who come to the sacrament in churches are just like the people who come to our annual dinner. They are there, as we are there, to share a common memory, a common gratitude, and a common loyalty.

They share a common memory, as we do at our meal.

By far the commonest phrase, when *we* meet, is "Do you remember so and so?" In just the same way, at Communion, we share a common memory. "Do this to remember . . ."

At our dinner we are a "fellowship" because we share the memory of our schooldays. At Communion we are a "fellowship" because we share the memory of Jesus.

And nothing does so much for any fellowship as the sharing of a common memory.

They share a common gratitude, as we do at our meal.

The more the years go on, the more we know that we owe so much to the training that we received more than forty years ago in our school. In just the same way at Communion, we share a common gratitude to Jesus because he gave himself for us, in his love.

They share a common loyalty, as we do at our meal.

At *our* dinner we still feel the tug of loyalty to Dalziel High School*, with its Latin motto: *Summa Petenda*. This really means, "Seek the Highest".

* Dr. Barclay's old school in Motherwell, Lanarkshire, Scotland.

At Communion we share a common loyalty to Jesus as our Lord and Master and we make our pledge to him once more.

A common memory, a common gratitude, a common loyalty—these are the things that bind men to each other and to Jesus Christ.

Read Acts 2: 41–47.

OUT OF PROPORTION   Day Seventeen

Do you ever use a magnifying glass?

I expect you do—for fun possibly, or perhaps in experiments at school, or to study stamps.

I like these magnifying glasses and I have written about them before (*Marching Orders*, page 32). They can be both useful and fun. But I don't like so much the magnifying glasses people seem to apply to quite other things—and I mentioned some things people do—like "magnifying" the harder parts of life, or carrying the whole world on their shoulders.

Here are some more things people do. There are some people who "magnify" harmless remarks they hear and turn them into harmful gossip.

There are people who take little incidents and "magnify" them into sensational news (some of our newspapers are inclined to do that sometimes!).

There are people who get upset about some comment made about them and "magnify" them into insults!

All this is really to lose our sense of proportion about life. We make trivial little things matter and this leads us, sometimes, to forget or ignore really important things.

Robert Louis Stevenson used to tell how, when he was a small boy, he found it hard to sleep because of illness. His nurse would then lift him from his cot and they would go to the window and, even in the middle of the night, they would see other windows with lights in them. Then they would tell each other that in these houses too, there were little boys and girls who were ill and who couldn't sleep.

In other words, it helps us when we remember that we are all bound up in "the bundle of life" and we are not the only people in trouble. It is part of being a human being.

We won't see so many slights and injuries in life, if we stop thinking of ourselves as if we were the centre of the universe, and if we think of other people's feelings as much as we think of our own!

Read James 4.

GOOD ADVICE   Day Eighteen

John Wycliffe was a great Bible translator.

Perhaps just because he knew *his* Bible so well, we should listen to his advice about how we can best understand the Bible.

Here it is:

"It will greatly help ye to understand the Scripture, if thou shalt mark, not only what is written, but by whom, and to whom, with what words, at what time, where, to what intent, with what circumstances, considering what goeth before and what followeth."

Centuries later, another great Bible scholar, F. J. A. Hort, said this in his introduction to his unfinished commentary on First Peter:

"To understand a book rightly, we want to know who wrote it, for what readers it was written, for what purposes, and under what circumstances."

This is good advice. It means that we can never really understand a book unless we understand something of the circumstances in which it was written, and something of the person who wrote it.

We can never fully appreciate a passage unless we take it within its context.

If you are going to understand the Bible, do all you can to find out about the times in which Jesus lived.

For example, we are used to shepherds following sheep, but a lot Jesus says about "the good shepherd" will not really come alive until we remember that the shepherds *he* knew *led* their sheep. If you read Psalm 23 in the light of that fact, how much more marvellous it becomes!

So learn all you can about Bible times. As Wycliffe says, it will help you to get even more out of our wonderful Bible!

Read Psalm 19.

WHO AND TO WHOM   Day Nineteen

It makes a difference also to know just who wrote particular words in the Bible.

Take the text, "My grace is sufficient for you" (2 Cor. 12: 8) for example. If someone had written that who had never experienced suffering, if it had been written by a man who had never known want or poverty or pain or toil, we might wonder what it really meant. But when we know that it was written by a man with a pain like a stake twisting in his body, and with a record of adventure that reads like an epic (2 Cor. 11: 23–28), then it really means something very important. St. Paul understood the meaning of grace, just because he had suffered so much. So what is said gains value from the man who said it.

It makes a difference too to know *to whom* particular words were written.

In 1 Corinthians 6: 9–11 Paul makes a list of certain sins and sinners. Then he writes, "And such were some of you." But now, he goes on, they are as "cleansed" as they were once "polluted".

The people to whom that was written lived in Corinth, and Corinth was the most wicked city in the ancient world. It was a city put out of bounds to Roman soldiers on leave because it was so dangerous and too full of temptation.

So all this means that if you say that God's "grace" can work in wicked situations and "be sufficient" there, you are saying something really wonderful about God.

Which is exactly what Paul was doing.

Read 2 Corinthians 13: 7–14.

WHERE AND WHEN   Day Twenty

It makes a difference too to know *where* particular words have been written.

The John who writes the Revelation begins the story of his vision like this: "I was on the isle called Patmos" (Rev. 1: 9).

Patmos was a little island to which criminals were sent to work in chain-gangs in the quarries. So it was actually in a convict settlement, in a chain-gang on a prison island, that there came to John one of the greatest visions that ever came to the mind of any man! You see, even in such a place as that a man can see the glory of God. Isn't that marvellous?

It makes a difference also to know *when* particular words were written.

"Fear God," Peter writes. "Honour the Emperor" (1 Pet. 2: 17).

Now that looks like a very ordinary command! *But who was the Emperor in question?*

If this letter is from the lips of the apostle Peter himself, then the Emperor in question is none other than Nero! So you must honour Nero, says Peter. Now that does seem strange. But what Peter is saying is that it is the duty of a Christian *to be a good citizen.* This he must be, not only when it is easy to do that, and when everything is in his favour, but also at a time when it is hard to be a good citizen and even when the state is hostile and cruel.

We must respect "the powers that be" even when they are unfriendly.

So you see that it does help to know when and where and all these sorts of things. In fact, the more we know about the Bible, the more wonderful its message is.

Read Revelation 1: 4–9.

THE RIGHT TIME   Day Twenty-one

If you play football, then you know how true it is that there is a right time to pass the ball, and a right time to "hold" it.

If you are a ballet dancer, you know how important "timing" is. It has got to be just right, hasn't it?

The ancient Preacher whose book we call Ecclesiastes (which means the Preacher), once said, "For every thing there is a season, and a time for every activity under heaven" (Ecc. 3: 1).

It is a useful rule of life to live "according to schedule". The time has come to do something. Whatever happens, do it!

If we wait for all the right conditions to come, the chances are that we shall never start at all.

When Paul talked to Felix in a way that alarmed Felix's soul, Felix told him to go away for the present, and he would send for him at a more convenient time (Acts 24: 25). But the "more convenient time" never came.

Felix never sent for Paul.

Put off a thing to a more convenient or favourable time, and the chances are that it will never be done.

213

There is something else to be said, however.

It is fatally easy to do things at the wrong time. To rush at something may be the worst thing to do.

One of the great skills in living is the art of choosing *the right moment* to do something.

We have to choose the right moment when to launch a scheme or a plan.

We have to choose the right moment when to speak to someone about something which is important.

There are many things which cannot be done by time-table or "on schedule". You need the ability to know when it is the right time to do them.

So the Preacher was right. There is a time for everything. We must avoid delay, evasion, the laziness that avoids action at the "right" time.

We have to avoid the recklessness and the haste that has neither the wisdom nor the patience to wait for the right moment.

If you can decide this matter, wisely, you will add a lot to your lives.

God knows the right time. For it was in the "fullness of the time"—at just the right moment, he sent Jesus.

Read St. John 1: 29–34.

HABIT Day Twenty-two

This incident happened in Canada to a friend of a friend of mine. It happened in the far north, and it happened at that time of year when the whole country was covered in snow.

Several people went for a walk together. The path they chose took them through a wood which was carpeted in snow and where every tree was like a Christmas tree.

One of them, a Canadian, was smoking a cigarette. He finished it and threw it on to the ground. But he very carefully crushed it with his foot until the smallest spark was finally extinguished.

One of the others, a visitor to Canada, looked on in astonishment and said, "Why on earth did you go to such trouble to extinguish your cigarette? The whole place is covered in snow. It could not possibly set anything alight. Why all this care?"

The Canadian replied, "If I came out here in the summertime and I dropped a lighted cigarette, the chances are I would cause a disastrous forest fire. So I have deliberately made it a habit never to drop a cigarette *anywhere* without making certain that it is really extinguished. So now I do it completely automatically."

That man had taught himself a very good habit, hadn't he?

Read 2 Timothy 2: 22–26.

THE PROMISE   Day Twenty-three

In Washington in the United States there is a Bible which once belonged to Abraham Lincoln. Lincoln used it all through the American Civil War.

There is a certain page in that Bible on which, if you look at it, you will see a soiled mark in the margin. It has clearly been caused by a finger being placed there again and again.

If you place your finger there you will find that it points to Psalm 34: 4. "I sought the Lord and he answered me, and delivered me from all my fears."

This is the text which helped Abraham Lincoln in very difficult times and he often turned to it.

I took out a book called *The Psalms in Human Life* by R. E. Prothero and I found that this thirty-fourth Psalm has been one of the great psalms in the spiritual experience of men.

For *William Law* it was one of these psalms which were so rich that he could feed upon it at any moment of the day.

The martyr *Theodore* was condemned to death because he had burned down the temple of the mother of the gods. As they tortured him, he found courage and strength by singing all the time, "I will bless the Lord at all times; his praise shall continually be in my mouth" (Psalm 34: 1).

When the saintly *John Fisher* was martyred in 1535, he was so ill that he could scarcely walk to the scaffold. As he climbed the steps, the sun suddenly shone. "Look to him," he whispered, "and be radiant" (Psalm 34: 5).

When *St. Columba* was dying, he was copying out the psalter, and he was in fact at this psalm. He came to the tenth verse, "The young lions suffer want and hunger; but those who seek the Lord lack no good thing."

"Here I make an end," he said, and laid down his pen for ever with the promise of God in his ears.

Read Psalm 34: 7–14.

THE "HOUSE" OF GOD   Day Twenty-four

The Church began in the house and the home. Paul never in his life preached in a "church" in the modern sense of the term! He preached either in a Jewish synagogue or in a Christian house and home.

Shouldn't our churches have more of the atmosphere and fellowship of houses and homes than they have?

For home is the place where we ought to feel we are close to one another. Our churches should be like that.

I sometimes wonder just what some of our buildings have become!

Some are so crowded with memorials and even tombs

216

that they feel like graveyards in stone rather than churches.

Some seem to have much more importance as ancient monuments than as churches.

Some are so elaborate in their worship that we find it difficult to understand what is happening.

Of course we want to have beautiful churches, but we want to be able to be at home in them.

So let's all do what we can to make churches more like houses and homes.

How about a buffet for example? Then we could meet for coffee and talk after the service. Some churches do this and I think it is of more value to the life of the congregation than all the stained glass windows we could get!

So let's make this one of *our* aims, churches where we can all feel "at home".

Read St. Mark 14: 12–26.

A CHRISTMAS BLESSING   Day Twenty-five

Julian Arnold is an Englishman who found himself all alone in Edinburgh on Christmas Eve.

He walked along the famous Princes Street, feeling very lonely. Then he went into a brightly-lit restaurant to eat a lonely dinner. He found a table and sat there all by himself. At the end of the meal, he summoned the waiter and asked for his bill.

The waiter said to him, "Sir, a gentleman sitting at a table nearby told me to tell you that he gathered from your accent that you were a stranger in our city, and therefore he had ventured to give himself the honour of being your unknown host upon this Christmas Eve. He hoped that you would pardon this wish of his to offer you his own good wishes, and the courtesy of his country."

A stranger's generosity lit up a lonely Christmas Eve for a stranger in a strange land.

You don't have to give money to be generous. Your

217

generosity can be expressed in the giving of your talents and, in fact, of yourself.

Bruno Walter, the famous musical conductor, tells how Kathleen Ferrier, that wonderful singer who died all too young, was in America. He himself had engagements in New York so he could not play host to her when she was in Los Angeles—as he would like to have done. He did then the only thing he could do. He gave her the use of his house in Los Angeles so that she might have comfort and peace there.

Bruno Walter goes on, "When we came home after she had left, our faithful domestic helpers, a married Austrian couple, told us that Kathleen, on her free evenings, used to call them to the music-room, where she sat down at the piano, shed her shoes, and sang to them to their heart's desire, and, of course, to their utter delight."

Generosity had been repaid in a marvellous way—by generosity to others.

You will never really lose by being generous.
Somewhere someone will be blessed.

Read 1 Corinthians 16: 1–9.

QUO VADIS?   Day Twenty-six

Quo Vadis?
Do you remember that famous Latin phrase? And the film of that name?
It simply means, "Where are you going?"
And that is an important thing to ask about life.
For it is having a real aim in life that will make it certain that you know where you are going!

You could ask this question over your studies.

Where are they leading you?
Where are you allowing them to take you?
To a dead-end job?
Or to the door that leads to success—in the best sense of the word?

What about your hobbies and your leisure activities?
Where are they leading you?
If anywhere!
Some hobbies can give you a lot of information. They can literally be part of your education.
That is good.
Often things you do in leisure time do nothing for you at all.
So they are really a waste of your time.

And your friendships?
Where do they take you?
In the right direction?
Or the wrong?

It is very important to ask this question "Where am I going?" when you are at *your* stage.
For there is every opportunity to change direction.

Read St. Luke 2: 33–40.

THE DOG   Day Twenty-seven

One of the loveliest legends about Jesus is the story of Jesus and the dead dog.

There was a crowd of people round a dead dog in a village in Galilee.
One said, "Look at his ragged ears; he was a fighter."
Another said, "Look at the bit of rope about his neck; he was a runaway."

Another said, "Look how dirty he is!"

Then from the edge of the crowd there came a voice, "Pearls are not whiter than his teeth."

The crowd turned round. "This," they said, "must be Jesus of Nazareth, for only he could find something good to say about a dead dog."

Jesus always found more to praise than to criticise.

It is so easy to be critical.

But criticism by itself is not the Christian way.

Read St. Luke 19: 28–38.

THE POWER FOR THE TASK   Day Twenty-eight

There are a lot of sayings that are said to be by Jesus but they are not in the Gospels. Here is one of these remarkable sayings:

"Raise the stone and thou shalt find me; cleave the wood and I am there."

It means that Jesus is there to help the mason as he dresses the stone. He is there to help the carpenter as he handles the wood.

None of us is ever left to work by ourselves. Jesus has promised to be with us to strengthen us and to help us whenever, after we have prayed, we follow prayer through in work and action.

That is why, time and time again, people have found it possible to do things which, humanly speaking, seemed impossible. That is why people have been ready to attempt tasks obviously beyond their powers. They have found the inspiration, the courage, and the strength in the knowledge that Jesus was there to help.

Jesus said to his disciples, "Go and teach all nations" (Matt. 28: 19).

He said to them, "You shall be witnesses unto me both in Jerusalem and in all Judaea and in Samaria and unto the uttermost part of the earth" (Acts 1: 8).

That was a command addressed to *no more than one hundred and twenty men*, as I have said earlier. And these were men without influence, without money, without learning, without prestige (Acts 1: 15). Yet these men set about that "impossible" task because Jesus had made another promise to them, "Lo, I am with with you always even unto the end of the world" (Matt. 28: 20).

With the task, there comes the power to do it.

Always.

Prayer and work must always go together.

"Pray without ceasing" and you will be able to work out great things for God.

Read St. Matthew 28: 16–20.

DO IT NOW! Day Twenty-nine

There is one habit that you should deliberately set out to acquire. It is the habit of "immediacy", the habit of doing things at once. For most things should be done at once or they won't be done at all.

When we are asked to do something, even the best of us will often say, "In a minute"; "Just let me finish reading or doing this and I'll do it"; "There's no hurry; there's plenty of time"; "It'll do perfectly well tomorrow." And so we delay and put off, and trouble sometimes comes.

To acquire the habit of doing things at once is one of the most valuable things you can do.

It is true of quite simple things, like answering letters and paying bills, and dealing with messages left for us.

It is true of things like paying visits. You may regret that

221

you did not go to see someone immediately, because that was the time they needed you.

It is true in the matter of giving help. The speed with which any appeal is answered adds much to the value of the answer.

As the Latin proverb we have quoted before has it, "He gives twice who gives quickly."

"Do it now" is a good rule in life, and a good resolution for a new year.

Read St. Matthew 21: 28–32.

SEE YONDER LIGHT?   Day Thirty

Do you recall the passage in John Bunyan's *Pilgrim's Progress* in which Bunyan described seeing Christian, when he couldn't make up his mind what to do?

Christian "looked as if he would run, yet he stood still, because, as I perceived, he could not tell which way to go."

Then Bunyan, in his dream, saw Evangelist come up to Christian, and say these famous words:

"Then," said Evangelist, pointing with his finger over a very wide field, "Do you see yonder wicket-gate?" The man said, "No." ... "Do you see yonder shining light?" Evangelist said. He said, "I think I do." "Then," said Evangelist, "Keep that light in your eye, and go up directly thereto, so shalt thou see the Gate; at which when thou knockest, it shall be told thee what thou shalt do."

We may not be sure, especially when we are young, of what we are aiming for, but we need have no doubt as to the direction in which we should be travelling.

The gate, Christian could not see. The light, he could see. By going towards the light, he would surely find the gate.

He knew the direction. For the time being, that was enough.

Keep moving towards the light.
You won't go far wrong if you do that.

Read St. John 12: 44–50.

DIRECTIONS   Day Thirty-one

Here is a question for the last day of the year!
What do you regard as "the right direction"?
Here are three possible answers!

The right direction can be *forward*.
When David Livingstone offered himself for missionary service, he was asked where he was willing to go.
"I will go anywhere," he said, "so long as it is forward."
It is a good new year resolution to go forward!

The right direction can be *outward*.
If we look *outward* instead of inwards, if we think of *others* instead of self, then life will be both more useful and happier.
In some places in Africa, when an African gets a very heavy load to carry, he puts it at one end of a pole. He then finds a stone of equal weight to the load and puts it on the other end of the pole. He then puts the pole with the load and stone across his shoulders and off he goes.
The stone balances the load, and that is much the easiest way to carry it.
In exactly the same way, the easiest way to carry troubles of our own is to carry someone else's troubles as well. If you are thinking about the troubles of others, you are much more likely to forget your own.

Read Hebrews 11: 32–12: 2.